Overcoming the Powers of Hell

Overcoming the Powers of Hell

John Miles & Beatrice Omese

New Wine Press

New Wine Ministries
PO Box 17
Chichester
West Sussex
United Kingdom
PO19 2AW

Copyright © 2009 John Miles & Beatrice Omese

All rights reserved. No part of this publication may be reproduced, stored in a retrieval system, or transmitted in any form or by any means, electronic, mechanical, photocopying or otherwise, without the prior written consent of the publisher. Short extracts may be used for review purposes.

Scripture quotations are taken from the following versions of the Bible: NIV – The Holy Bible, New International Version. Copyright © 1973, 1978, 1984 by International Bible Society. Used by permission of Hodder and Stoughton Limited.

ISBN 978-1-905991-42-6

Typeset by **documen**, www.documen.co.uk
Cover design by CCD, www.ccdgroup.co.uk
Printed in Malta

Dedication

For Grace,
who invariably lives up to her name.

About the author

John Miles has worked in missions in many nations of the world and until recently was Director for Africa for the missions organisation *International Teams*. John has a Masters Degree in Missions from the Birmingham Bible Institute. He is married to Grace and they have three children.

Acknowledgements

My thanks to our great friends Paul and Tessa Settatree. They are the inspiration behind both this book and the powerful Christian ministry described within. They are a fine example of how a Christian family can have an effective ministry in Africa while maintaining a home, a business and family life back home in West Wales. They conducted the video interviews for chapter seven while on one of their many visits to Soroti.

Thanks to my wife Grace, who read and re-read the text several times, making corrections and useful suggestions as always.

Thanks to The Sentinel Group for their DVD, *An Unconventional War*. It is an excellent source of information and pointed me in the right direction for further research on numerous occasions. I highly recommend this powerful film to anyone interested in the real nature of the conflict in Northern Uganda. It can be obtained from: www.TransformNations.com

Contents

Chapter 1	Mother of Woes	13
Chapter 2	An African Girl	21
Chapter 3	Conceived in Hell	31
Chapter 4	Big John	35
Chapter 5	Evil Descending	43
Chapter 6	Long Way Down	55
Chapter 7	Survivors, Eyewitnesses and the Lives of Others	63
Chapter 8	New Life and Near Death	73
Chapter 9	The Power of Forgiveness	79
Chapter 10	The Ministry Begins	89
Chapter 11	Evil at the Door	97
Chapter 12	The Promise of God	105
Chapter 13	The Calling of God	115
Chapter 14	God's Answer	127
Chapter 15	Victory Over the Darkness	137
Chapter 16	Epilogues	149

Mother of Woes

CHAPTER 1

Beatrice Omese

The tragic news that came to Beatrice Omese one afternoon in 1999 came in a very African way. Sadly, untimely death is common in Africa. No more so than in Beatrice's home area of northern Uganda. For decades, violence, insurgency, roaming gangs of robbers, soldiers and rustlers have killed, raped, tortured and abducted countless thousands of the population. African cultures have had to accommodate the fact that death comes frequently and often suddenly. The town of Soroti where Beatrice Omese lives, with a population of 60,000, has escaped much of the most recent turmoil, located as it is in the southern part of their troubled Teso tribal region.

It was about five in the afternoon and Beatrice had been taking a nap. That she was six months pregnant would in itself be a good reason for a rest, but added to this, Beatrice had worked the morning tending the large patch of vegetables that helped support the small Bible College run by her husband, Pastor John Omese. It was called "Vision Bible College". Her advanced stage of pregnancy, the back-breaking work and the merciless heat of the African sun, all ensured that she had slept soundly throughout the afternoon.

As she awoke, the crying of her youngest son Joshua demanded her attention; he was hungry and needed milk. She went to warm some for him and saw that a group of local pastors were waiting for her on the veranda. One of them, Pastor Charles, seeing she was now awake, crept in and spoke softly to her. "We are waiting outside and we have something to tell you – when you have finished what you are doing."

This was nothing unusual; her husband John often had other local pastors coming to see him. Their house was usually a centre of activity, meetings and a place where people would just show up hoping for some help. She told Charles that she would be with them in a moment and went to feed Joshua.

Once Joshua had been settled, she went out to see the three pastors. All were men she knew well. She could see immediately from their body language and their faces that all was not well – it must be bad news. One of the coping mechanisms that Africans have is to break bad news gradually and as gently as possible. Beatrice greeted each one with a brief handshake as normal, wondering what the matter was. "What is the problem?" she asked them guardedly.

The enquiry was met with silence and they sat looking at the floor. This warned her that it must be very bad news for them to act in this way. Pastor Charles said, "John has had an accident, the news is not good and you must take heart."

It was the part about "taking heart" that set her heart racing and fear began to envelop her. She knew that John was out of town riding a motorcycle which he had hired for the day. Her mind suddenly became her tormentor. *"Oh no, John must be very seriously injured or, God help me, even dead!"*

Now Beatrice became more insistent. "You tell me now, what is his condition – please tell me the truth, don't beat around the bush." Again she was met with silence and eyes averted. Now came the shocking thought that her wonderful, strong, six feet six tall, dynamic John, surely must be dead or the pastors would not be acting in this way. It was their culture not to blurt out such tragic news quickly.

She went back into the house, her head spinning, wondering what she should do next. She must find out what had happened. If these good men could not bring themselves to tell her, she must find out for herself. She left the house and passed thought the gate of the compound, not really knowing where she was going or what she would do. Her first thought was that she should check the hospital to see if John was there. As she passed through the gate, a close friend of John's was approaching in his car. This was another Pastor John, who led the Baptist church in Soroti and was a senior pastor in the town, well regarded by all.

Because he had a car, he had recovered John's body from the accident site near town and taken it to the hospital. Now he was coming from the hospital to tell Beatrice the bad news. His seniority and closeness to John meant that he had to take the responsibility of telling Beatrice the awful news.

He got out of his car and looked Beatrice in the eye. Realising that she was probably hurrying to the hospital he said, "My daughter, your husband is already dead and I want you to have the peace of God." Then he prayed for her.

"Where are you going now, my daughter?" he asked.

"I want to go and see him."

"They won't allow you to see him. They are doing the post mortem now."

"Then please take me to see Donald."

Donald Hemmingway and his wife were visiting Soroti at that time. Donald was a retired Elim Pentecostal minister from New Zealand and he had been helping John with funding to establish his ministry. He had helped to raise funds for John and Beatrice to go to Bible College and was now assisting in establishing the small Bible College in Soroti that John was leading. Donald had been close to her and John and she wanted to be the one to break the news to him. They were, of course, just as shocked as everyone else. They had invested a lot in John and his ministry. Now they must have wondered what would become of it. Would it all end with this terrible accident? Would the big vision that this big man, Pastor John Omese, had for Soroti die with him? Actually, nothing would be further from the truth.

Over the next few hours and days Beatrice was able to piece together the events of that fateful afternoon. John had just returned from a Pastors' conference in Nairobi organised by Assemblies of God (AOG) workers from the UK. He was able to travel to and from this conference by bus. Returning after a week away, he was eager to visit the various projects he was developing in the area. John was a man in a hurry; a week was a long time in his life; he lived with a sense of urgency. He was also organising a Pastors' conference locally. He was simultaneously starting a secretarial training school, a secondary school in Soroti, another Bible college and, thirty miles north of Soroti, a secondary school in the large village of Otuboi . This was John's ancestral village and his father and extended family lived there. It is in the heart of the Teso tribal area. Like most Africans, he wanted to do something good for his own people. An African who achieves success is expected to do their best to share some of that success with his own family and home village if possible.

To get round and see them all in a day he needed a vehicle. Going by public transport would take too long, so he hired a motor cycle. He had long wanted to own one, but in the meantime he had to content himself with borrowing. His final call of the day was to Otuboi to meet with the teachers and students and see how the school, Trinity College, was progressing. On his return journey he was asked to give one of the teachers a lift home. It was a small motor cycle for someone as big as John and with a passenger it was asking a lot. It had been raining and the roads were treacherous and muddy. Near to Soroti, John had turned off the main road to visit a friend, Pastor Justin Elaneu, who was sick. They needed to discuss the Pastors' conference they were organising. The side road was in poor condition, full of large potholes filled with muddy water. The problem with potholes filled with water is that you can't tell how deep they are. Africans become adept at dodging potholes, but John was not a regular motorcyclist and the small machine carried two, making it difficult to control in the treacherous conditions. He did his best to swerve round the worst holes. Unfortunately, one caught him by surprise; the motor cycle lurched and the passenger fell off, suffering injuries as he hit the road and rolled. Struggling both to regain control of the bike and avoid more potholes, John hit a large one and the front wheel crashed into it, stopping the bike with a jolt. John's enormous frame flew over the handlebars and hit a tree head first. Not owning a crash helmet, John suffered fatal head injuries and died at the accident site.

Friends and family all gathered round to make the arrangements for what would inevitably be a large funeral for John. He was well known as a young, dynamic pastor with lots of vision. He was not content with one project, he had at least four all being developed together. Many people came to the funeral, held in the largest church building available.

It is the custom in Africa for the widow to sit and mourn for several days at her home. Friends and family come and sit with the widow, mostly in silence and share the grief. The length of time they stay depends on how close they were to the deceased. Every new person that enters the room will receive an explanation of the circumstances of the death and what led up to it. Some modern psychologists who have studied this custom think this is a very effective way of dealing with grief. It may explain why so many Africans seem to recover quickly from the death of a loved one and resume life as best they can. The fact that sudden death is so common in Africa may also be part of the story.

It was a devastating fact that John's life had come to a sudden and premature end. He had been well trained and he was ready to employ his boundless energy to do great things for God. What would now happen to the work he had begun? He had been the driving force behind it all.

For Beatrice, the thoughts and emotions were perhaps different to most widows in similar circumstances in the West. There was the same grief, shock and deep sense of loss. Alongside this was concern about her future. In Uganda, as with most of Africa, there is no state support for families without an income. How would they manage to buy food, pay rent on their house, or pay school fees?

In their culture, widows are at the bottom of the social and economic scale. In the midst of this worry and sense of loneliness, immediately the word of God came to her heart telling her not to worry, she was not alone; to rejoice in all circumstances and He would care for her and her family. This word from God was hard to believe, but she took great strength from it.

A typical widow. Her face is a mixture of sadness and determination.

At the funeral she was strong. Many acquaintances thought she would "collapse and die", but she didn't and was a source of strength for other friends and family members. The funeral was conducted by AOG minister Revd. John Akanyu, who, now retired, had married them. He conducted the service but asked the indulgence of the congregation to excuse him for not preaching any sermon. He explained that he was so grief-stricken that he had no words. Unusually in their culture, Beatrice was asked if she wanted to say something to the congregation. Her words to the packed church were remarkable:

> "The devil thinks that by taking my husband, he will get me down, but this is the time that I am going to show the devil that I am with God and I am going to preach the Gospel. I had already promised God that when I am thirty, I will preach the Gospel. I am now twenty-nine years old and I had already told my husband that after thirty, I wanted no more children because I want to preach the Gospel full time. I want to see God use me in the ministry of His Word. I am not ready to backslide. I am going to be on fire for Jesus."

Now the congregation were encouraged and began to praise and thank God. Even the Revd. John Akanyu said that he was now encouraged and now had some words to say.

It is customary in many African cultures for the family of the husband who dies to come and snatch all the possessions that the couple have gathered over the years. The house will be stripped bare and the widow and her children left destitute. Some African governments, including Uganda, have now outlawed this practice, but it is still widespread. Widows become pariahs in their community. People avoid them for fear of getting involved in their problems. In African culture, it is customary to help others in trouble if you can, particularly if they are related in any way. People are torn because they have enough problems of their own to cope with. They just do not have the means to help widows. Their solution is to avoid them. If they never hear from the widow about her problems, they do not feel guilty or embarrassed about not helping her. Some will even cross the street if they see a widow they know coming towards them. They have an expression in the Teso language for widows, it literally means, *mother of problems.*

This did not happen to Beatrice because her family were Christians and more supportive. However, her family were not wealthy; their help was limited and the future loomed large in her mind. There was a heavy rent to pay for their house. The owner of the house was a widow herself. She was sympathetic and patient, waiting for the rent. However, she depended on that rent to keep herself and family. Beatrice had three sons and a fourth in her womb, soon to be delivered. At twenty nine, she was still young, attractive, intelligent, educated and full of talent that was yet to be revealed. Throughout the trauma of the last few days she had experienced a strange peace, deep in her heart, that she knew was from God. To everyone's surprise, she was even able to comfort and encourage others at the funeral. Nevertheless, as she looked down the dark tunnel of her future, she faced the dawning reality that now she too was a widow, *a mother of problems.*

CHAPTER 2

An African Girl

Beatrice was ten years old in 1980 when the first big change in her life took place. Her father, Simon Peter Enotu, left their family home in the village of Amuria, not far from Soroti, and moved to Soroti town and married a second wife. This was not very unusual in their culture, but it was a low point in the family's history. He moved to pursue various business interests and to try to improve his financial situation. Beatrice was the oldest of the children and had three sisters and a brother. Her youngest sister was only a toddler.

This meant that a lot of responsibility was now on her young shoulders. All the burden of the farming and raising the animals now fell to her mother. Beatrice took over many of the family chores – washing clothes, cooking meals, cleaning the house and bathing the younger children. Even after she moved into town for schooling, she still performed these tasks whenever she came home. Saturday was always her busiest day of the week. The workload naturally affected her school work and she didn't do quite as well as she knew she could. In later life, this early responsibility bore fruit. It helped to mould her personality and enhance her leadership ability.

Of this period she now recalls, "I was a mother at ten years of age."

Even her father's abandoning of his family had some beneficial effects in the long term. At the age of eleven, Simon Peter decided that Beatrice should leave their village and attend a Catholic boarding school in Soroti town. They were fortunate that their village had a school. Village schools are not always very good in Africa. They often lack equipment and books and are usually overcrowded. The Teso tribal region of Uganda has a proud history of academic achievement, usually supplying more teachers and professional workers than other areas of their country.

Like most Africans, Beatrice's family had a great thirst for education. Education is the way to advancement and a good job. It is at school that you learn English. Ateso, spoken by nearly a million people in Northern Uganda, would always be their beloved mother tongue, but everyone knows that to get on in life, you must be educated in English. As with many other countries it is a colonial heritage that cannot be changed. It is not uncommon for African children to walk for two or three hours to reach the nearest school. Simon Peter soon realised that Beatrice was intelligent, consistently coming top of her class. He was determined that the village school was not going to be the limit of his children's education. Beatrice could, of course, stay in the village school, continue to help her mother on the family plot, marry young and have lots of children. This was traditional life in an African village. If the rains come regularly, if sudden death doesn't strike, and they were not attacked by the Karamajong tribe – who were murderous cattle rustlers – then life was happy in the village.

Simon Peter had developed a few small business interests in Soroti and he began to look at the private schools in town. Could he afford the fees? Were they a good standard? Were the children well cared for? In his visits to town he had made the acquaintance of Sister Ruth, who taught at the Catholic boarding school. Hearing Simon Peter's plan, she enthusiastically recommended her school for his two oldest daughters. More than that, she assured him that she personally would see that the girls had everything they needed. She would be their guardian angel in the school. This was the assurance that Simon Peter was looking for; his lovely daughter would be safe, well fed and protected. After all, it was a church school. The school was a joint venture with the government, but the staff were people of faith who surely had moral standards. He was happy to have found a good school and by working hard, he thought he could afford the fees. It was a big event for Beatrice who was followed later by her younger sister, Mary. No one in their family had ever taken this important step and moved out of their ancestral village. The whole community buzzed with the news.

Beatrice set off, carrying her small bag of clothes, most important of which was the treasured school uniform. Soroti must have seemed like a large city with a population of 60,000 in comparison to her village. The main street of Soroti is lined with buildings from another era. Some are clearly showing their age and were constructed in the colonial era. They might have dates such as "1918" embossed on their facade. The main road through town is surprisingly wide. As in many other towns and even capital cities in Africa such as Harare, the roads were built wide enough to allow a team of six or eight oxen pulling a heavy wagon to do a U-turn. Others are of eastern flavour and were built by the Asian traders that were eventually expelled by Idi Amin. Along most of the street you can walk under the shade of a veranda built onto the front of the shops. Public transport around town is mainly by "Boda Boda". These are simply bicycles with a padded passenger seat on the back. The passenger sits astride the seat or side-saddle if it is a lady and the owner pedals hard in the hot African sun to deliver their passenger. His reward is a few shillings and by working long hours he can support his family at a very basic level. They weave precariously between a mass of trucks and minibus taxis that take people to outlying villages and other towns.

Unfortunately, shortly after moving to the school, their friend and mentor, Sister Ruth was transferred to another school. This combined with falling standards meant that life at the school turned out to be far less pleasant than anyone had anticipated!

Beatrice looked in horror at her lunch plate. At first she couldn't believe it, but there were definitely maggots in her food! She turned to her sister Mary sitting next to her and in a hushed voice said, "Mary, there are maggots in my food."

"Mine is the same, but I have removed a couple and I am trying to eat because I am hungry."

"Mary, I can't eat food with maggots in it, even if I am hungry!"

"But Beatrice, what will you eat?"

"I don't know, but I am sorry, I just can't eat this, I will be sick."

Conditions at the Catholic boarding school in Soroti had never been good; the food was generally poor, but this was far worse. They were usually fed with "relief" food donated by aid agencies. Of course, this was not what the food was donated for. They were in a private school and their father paid fees for them. He gave them only a small amount of pocket money because he believed that all their needs would be met. Beatrice now spent this small amount on tea and small quantities of food; she just could not eat rotten food.

Eventually, even Mary gave up trying to eat the food. One day Mary came late for class. She had discovered that in the school there was a supply of ground nuts in the store. She was so hungry that she sneaked off and helped herself to some of the nuts. What she had done was soon discovered. This meant punishment.

Discipline in the school was harsh by Western standards. The usual punishment was to lie face down on the floor and be beaten with a stick on the buttocks, in front of the class. For minor offences it was three strokes and seven for more serious offences such as this. For very serious offences, even twenty strokes were permissible. Beatrice only remembers receiving three strokes herself. It wasn't just naughtiness that received punishment; poor academic performance was also considered an offence. Once, Beatrice was punished for getting only three of her sums correct out of ten. She was a bright girl and the teacher considered this to be a lack of effort and concentration that required punishment. She was supposed to have seven strokes of the dreaded cane. She was last in the line of children to be beaten and the more she watched the punishment being meted out to the others, the more afraid she became and she started crying. This made the teacher relent and he told her that she was forgiven and there was no punishment on this occasion. The other children protested and asked why only Beatrice was forgiven. Africans have a saying: "What doesn't kill us makes us stronger." Beatrice was now even more determined to do well at her studies and use the keen mind that God had given her.

When Simon Peter heard of the deterioration in the school's standards he removed his daughters and placed them in a day school in the town. Being educated at a Catholic boarding school had a status attached to it, but he wasn't going to allow his daughters to suffer these very poor standards. Beatrice's academic work improved in the day school and she became one of the best students. She and her sister were now getting better food. Simon Peter's second wife stayed in a house in town and cooked better food for the girls. Beatrice's mother stayed in the village and took care of the farming on their family plot. The second marriage lasted long enough for two sons and two daughters to be born before the second wife left and married someone else.

When subsequent marriages take place, the new husband usually doesn't want the children that his wife has from a previous marriage. Likewise, the husband from the first marriage doesn't want to lose his children; they are his security for old age. Until they are adults, he is responsible for them. He has the responsibility of their education and making the arrangements for their marriages later. Negotiating the size of the dowry, how lavish the wedding celebration will be and where it will take place, is all the responsibility of the father. In Africa, informal marriages are often made for economic or even survival reasons. The ceremony for the second marriage was a traditional one conducted in the village where Simon Peter was raised. Just as important is the fact that the children also belong to the village of the father. They are part of that community and will be for the rest of their lives, regardless of where they go or live. It will always be *their village*. An African saying that has become popular to quote in the West is, "It takes a village to raise a child". There is a deep cultural truth behind this. We have no real equivalent in the West to the sense of belonging and ties of ownership that exist between an African and the village that they or their parents were born and raised in. If at all possible, it is that same village where they wish to be buried, on the family land with their ancestors.

Multiple wives are very common in places such as rural Mozambique. Sixteen years of civil war caused many of the men to flee the country or die in the fighting. The result is that most men in the villages have three or four wives. The system works well in the harsh conditions of life in the bush. The male view is often that a man needs one wife to look after the children, one to fetch water (an exhausting task that can take most of the day), one to do the cooking and look after the animals and one to cultivate the plot. What does the husband do? He might do a little fishing or hunting. The rest of the time he will discuss important issues of life with the other men of the village under a shady tree, ensure there are plenty of babies and generally manage his domestic team.

Beatrice's spiritual development began in childhood. In common with almost all Africans, she didn't need to be convinced about the existence of God and that one day she would have to give account to Him for her life. Even as a child of eleven, she was conscious of God speaking to her. She often had dreams. She once dreamed that a train was taking people to heaven. She was watching the train depart and she was left standing there.

"Why have I been left behind?" she asked.

Someone standing near said, "It is because you have not given your life to Christ."

Then she woke up. But this was more than a natural waking from sleep. She awoke knowing that she must give her life to Christ and become His follower. Her best friend at the time was Esther, who was herself already a Christian. Esther used to tell her about her own Christian faith and often said to her, "Beatrice, it is time for you too to give your life to Christ."

Beatrice would reply, "Yes, I will eventually, I am just taking my time."

Some adult friends she knew would also talk to her about becoming a Christian. A family friend, Santos John Labeja, and Pastor Isaac, one of the local ministers, both had serious conversations with her at different times during her teenage years and encouraged her to decide to live her life for Christ. Many of her friends were already Christians. In another dream, she was conscious of fading light and growing darkness.

One of her friends was looking down to her and saying, "Beatrice, come up here."

"I can't see the way, it is too dark down here."

"But Beatrice, it isn't dark, I can see you clearly. It is you who is in the dark."

"But Esther, I can't even move an inch, please come and hold my hand so that I can find the way."

"Beatrice, this is why I have been telling you to give your life to Christ. Then you also will be able to see the light."

At this point she woke up. In another dream she saw fire and it was filling the earth. The fire was coming from a certain direction and she was running from it, but it still followed her and she was crying with fear. Again at this point she awoke. She realised that God was speaking to her through the dreams. If she didn't give her life to the Lord, she would burn. This was an attention grabbing thought by any standards!

She already owned a Bible that one of her many Christian friends had given her. She was in the habit of reading it before she got out of bed in the mornings. She didn't read it systematically, but just opened it at random and read whatever was on that page.

Her early teenage years passed in this way. Always intending to give her life to Christ, but always being aware that she needed to make that final commitment and surrender entirely to God. She continued reading her Bible and praying regularly, even fasting. One morning, she opened her Bible at the book of Proverbs, to a place where it said, *"Do not make rash promises."* She realised at that point that she had been promising God that she would become a Christian, but not keeping the promise. It was better not to make the promise than to do so and not keep it. That God was speaking to her was confirmed later that day while visiting her grandfather's house in town. Pastor Isaac from the Pentecostal Faith Church came to visit her grandfather. Her grandfather loved her very much and was really proud of her. When Isaac entered the house her grandfather introduced her, saying that she was his first granddaughter and was doing well at school and had come to stay with him for the holiday period. Pastor Isaac took an interest in her and began to tell her about Christ. He asked her, "Have you given your life to Christ yet?"

"I am going to." She replied.

"When are you going to?"

"I am an Anglican, so when I do, it will be in an Anglican church," she explained. Perhaps she thought that Isaac was trying to gain another member for his congregation.

But he said to her, "It's all right, I am not trying to tell you to come to our church. It doesn't matter which church, so long as you give your life to Christ."

This made an impact on Beatrice. She realised just how powerfully God was speaking to her. "Tomorrow I will go to our church and give my life to God," she said. Isaac warned her not to lie about it. However, she insisted that she was serious.

"That's all right then," Isaac said with a kindly smile on his face.

It was a Saturday and she would be going to church the next day anyway. The next morning in church, her father and grandfather were observing her with more interest than usual. Her grandfather believed that she was already a Christian because of the Christian lifestyle that she led. It was only Beatrice that knew deep down that she still had to give herself fully to Christ. This would be a major turning point in her life and once she made her long-delayed commitment, it would be decisive and there would be no turning back.

The speaker was Revd. Isodo, who was a minister visiting their church from a nearby town. He spoke from Mark 8:36: "*What shall it profit a man if he gain the whole world but lose his soul?*" He made an altar call and as he did so, he sang a song to the congregation. The theme of the song was that this world is so difficult that when we go to Heaven we will really praise God for our deliverance. It is a concept particularly apt for Africans.

She briefly thought about her life so far and realised that this was now the time to make her final and complete commitment. From now on it was going to be Christ and Him alone that she would live for. She rose from her seat in the middle of the church and was the first one to reach the front. Tears of genuine repentance streamed down her face. This was the real thing. About twenty others in the congregation came forward to join her, kneeling in front of the altar. The minister prayed for them all. The Revd. Isodo was a charismatic Anglican and preached the need for salvation.

That evening, Pastor Isaac came round to the house to check if she had carried through her promise to commit herself that morning. She told him she had and they both rejoiced. Her grandfather insisted that she had been a Christian all along. Her lifestyle, her good behaviour and her many Christian friends had convinced him that she was already saved. Beatrice knew two truths; first that she needed to make a further commitment and secondly that she had now done so. From now on, whatever school, college, society or club she joined, she was elected to be the leader by her contemporaries. This was partly because she was an outstanding Christian, but also because she had that almost indefinable African gift of natural leadership.

At the age of sixteen Beatrice had graduated from her secondary school and was sent to a technical school in the nearby district of Katakwi to study tailoring for three years. To have a skill is highly prized. You can support a family with such a skill. A girl has more status in the marriage stakes if she is educated and has family income-generating potential. Beatrice did well at her studies, taking an advanced diploma to become a tutor in Madera Technical Institute in Soroti at the age of only nineteen. This college taught building and carpentry, but until Beatrice arrived on the scene had never taught tailoring. Beatrice had to design the course and write the syllabus, which then had to be approved by the education authorities. Adding tailoring to the curriculum of the college was important because it gave an opportunity for young women as well as young men to gain a skill. She had not been at Madera very long before she was elected as leader of the Christian Union in the college.

Beatrice was now several steps up the social and economic ladder from being a village girl, thanks to her own hard work and the ambition of her father that his children would get the chance to make a good life beyond the confines of the traditional village existence. Add to this her good looks, wealth of talent, a ready smile, and she had become a very eligible young lady indeed. Studying at Kyambogo University in Kampala for her teaching diploma would have been her next step, but something intervened that was to radically change the course of her life – marriage.

CHAPTER 3

Conceived in Hell

In 1987, when Beatrice was just eighteen years old, a dark and evil cloud which had its genesis in hell itself, settled over northern Uganda. It began a reign of terror so vile that it would shock the entire world. At first, to the outside world, it looked like a typical African war. Some jumped-up warlord had gathered a group of thugs around him, then been armed by trouble-making elements in their northern neighbouring country, Sudan. These people then began attacking Teso's neighbours, the Acholi people, in the northernmost district of Uganda. For those who really knew what was happening, it was far more sinister that that. In fact, it was to be a demonstration of just how low humankind can sink when under the influence and even total possession of powerful demonic beings. It was a terror that would eventually engulf both the Acholi and most of the Teso areas.

Northern Uganda has been an area of unusually high demonic activity for many generations. The area has a history of witchcraft and sorcery that spawned almost every kind of evil that mankind has experienced. In folklore and documentation there are accounts of violence, rape, mutilation, burning, torture, robbery, slavery, abduction, child sacrifice, cannibalism and, as always, the all-pervading corruption that blights so much of Africa. Just a few weeks ago, while writing this book, a Ugandan friend of the author had his four year old boy abducted and ritualistically murdered – sacrificed to the spirits. This is not mythology, it is real! In return for surrendering their lives to Satan, the sorcerers and practitioners of witchcraft gain power to do supernatural things that impress and cause fear in others. For scriptural examples of this see Exodus 7:11 and 22.

However, there is always a price to pay, and that is usually blood. Much more could be written about this, but it is preferred not to elaborate on the works of evil. What can be said is that if the secret details of the higher levels of sorcery were to be written, most readers would simply be unable to believe most of the things that go on under the power of evil spirits. The Western trivialising of things such as Halloween and witches, even in the church, show that Satan has been very successful in convincing most of the Western world that he is figure of fun – when just the opposite is true. The one laughing the loudest on October 31st is always Satan himself!

We know from the Bible that there are many kinds of evil spirits, also known as demons. One of the types that the Bible particularly warns us about are those that empower false prophets and false teachers. Some biblical scholars refer to these as "religious spirits". These were the spirits that empowered the heart of this movement in Northern Uganda. Many other evil powers would be swept along in its train, but it was essentially a religious cult. Its name confused many who did not know its religious nature. It was called "The Lord's Resistance Army", often referred to as "The LRA".

The Bible tells us, even in the Ten Commandments, that

"The sins of the parents are visited on their children to the third and fourth generation"

(Exodus 20:5).

The outpouring of evil that accompanied the LRA incursions into northern Uganda did not have its origin with their leader Joseph Kony. We have to go back to a shadowy cult leader called Severino Lukoya. His movement was small, but religious in character. He claimed to be possessed by seventy-one spirits. The leader and most powerful of this spirit group would loudly proclaim, "I am the Spirit of God the Father."

His powers were passed on to his daughter, a former prostitute, Alice Auma, born January 2nd 1956. She took the movement to a new level, calling it *The Holy Spirit Movement.*

In a witchcraft ceremony she invited a powerful religious spirit called *Lakwena,* which means messenger or apostle in the Acholi language, to possess her. She soon became known as Alice Lakwena. As a result of the ceremony she went mad and was unable to hear or speak. Her father took her to eleven witchdoctors for a cure, but all failed. They had their own proven powers, but none could touch the powerful demon that Alice had invited into her spirit. It is said that she was then guided by the spirit to the Murchison Falls National Park. It is said that here she disappeared for forty days beneath the waters of the River Nile, only to re-emerge as a "spirit medium" and set up her base near Gulu.

She began to gather a lot of devoted followers, up to 10,000 at the movement's height. Her followers called her "Your Holiness". She is said to have had the power to heal AIDS and give sight to the blind. With her rag-tag army she rebelled against the government. She convinced her fighters that if they smeared "Holy Oil" over their bodies they would be immune to bullets. Also, the rocks they threw would become grenades in flight. They ran into battle, high on drugs, wearing witchcraft amulets and trinkets, clapping and singing. Her fighters were mown down by the modern weapons of the Uganda People's Defence Force, thus providing the blood that she was required to deliver as her part of the covenant which she had made with Satan while in the national park. Her reward for the covenant was receiving supernatural power. She was finally stopped near the town of Jinja in central Uganda, barely an hour's travel from the capital Kampala. People followed her because of her healing powers. However, all such healings are conditional. There is always a price to pay. The same sickness, or some other, comes back later, worse. Alternatively, the patient suffers mental breakdown or moral debauchery. In these covenants, of which there are many in the world, there is only one winner and it is never the patient! The aim of the whole system is always the same – premature death.

At the time of her defeat, Professor Isaac Newton Ojok was her deputy. He had formerly been a lecturer at Makerere University before becoming Minister of Education in Milton Obote's second administration after Idi Amin was ousted by Tanzanian forces in 1979. Education and intelligence have never been any obstacle to man's involvement in witchcraft. Alice fled to a refugee camp in Kenya and died in January 2007 of unknown causes – her time was up. She now had her own price to pay for the evil life she had chosen to live.

We would all wish it had ended there. Unfortunately, a new personality took on the satanic family mantle. Her young cousin Joseph Kony, a high school dropout, stepped up to cut his own deal with the devil. With each generation the spiritual inheritance becomes more powerful, until its course is run and ends with the third or fourth generation, or God steps in to put an end to it. The power he wielded and the resulting evil was beyond anything so far seen. As Joseph Kony strode to centre stage, northern Uganda trembled and the world looked on in horror.

CHAPTER 4

Big John

John Omese was typical of many men of the Iteso tribe; he was six feet six inches tall and he had a personality to match his giant frame. Even the Iteso women are often very tall. The tribe had originally migrated around 1600 AD from the harsh mountain terrain of Ethiopia. When they reached the area that today is north east Uganda, the tribe decided to divide. The families headed by older men were finding the trek very hard and too many were dying along the way. The young men of the tribe mocked the faintheartedness of the old men and called them "old women", which is *karamajong* in their language, and so this became their tribal name. The older men warned the younger ones that if they travelled any further, they would die. Their word for this was *teso* and, likewise, this became their name. They migrated a little further south west to where they are today in the region that bears their tribal name, Teso. Ironically, the section of the tribe that was left behind became the feared Karamajong tribe, Teso's cattle rustling enemies. They brought few cattle with them and these mostly belonged to the older men. This gave rise to the necessity to become good farmers, getting the best from the more fertile and well-watered soil on which they now lived. The combination of their expertise in farming and raising cattle has ensured that the Iteso tribe would prosper and could afford schooling for many of their children, making them probably the most educated tribe in the region.

John was a natural leader. He became a pastor eventually, but he would have been a leader in whatever he chose to do in life. In Africa, natural leadership ability is encouraged to develop from childhood if a boy or even a girl has that type of character. In Western countries, if a junior school teacher is asked who is the leader among the boys in their class, and likewise among the girls, they will instantly be able to tell you. In the West, we usually then overlay this natural development with the requirement for training and academic qualifications. This sometimes results in managers of commerce or industry who are given their position because of academic achievements, but who perform poorly because they are not natural leaders.

Both John and Beatrice's life now began to run on parallel courses which meant that eventually they would meet. Both had this natural leadership quality. Both were teaching in Soroti, John in a local senior secondary school. Both were developing in their Christian faith. Both were elected by their peers as "Patrons" – similar to the role of prefects in British schools. They were elected leaders of the Christian Union in their respective places of work. One could say that they were meant for each other.

It was the custom for the various Christian Unions from schools and colleges in Soroti to meet together once a month for combined fellowship. This is where they met. They couldn't really miss each other because they both regularly preached or gave testimony in the meetings. It was hard to miss John because he towered over most other people. John, at twenty-six, was in his second year as a teacher in the government run Soroti Secondary School. He taught geography and history. He had trained at Nagogera National Teacher Training College in Tororo district. There was a Christian Union among the teachers from the schools in the region and they too met together regularly. John was elected as Chairman of this group by his fellow Christian teachers – he was an outstanding leader. At this stage of his life, he was naturally thinking about marriage. Suddenly, before his eyes, was the perfect girl: Beatrice. She had everything that he wanted in a wife. Beautiful, intelligent, she was even a spiritual leader, well respected by all her friends and colleagues. He also noticed that she was the one her friends went to for spiritual advice. He was smitten.

⁂

It was not a typical arranged marriage – they met and fell in love, but the marriage had to be arranged by their families. John and Beatrice broke the news to their families. As a modern educated couple, they were asking for a blessing rather than their permission. Their fathers needed to make the arrangements, which included agreeing the all-important dowry.

The long tradition of the Iteso tribe was that their wealth was measured in cattle. Simon Peter could have expected to receive a good dowry of cattle for each of his daughters. This tradition has been under pressure since the 1980s when the Karamajong tribe had begun trading some of their cattle across the border of Sudan in exchange for AK47 rifles. In most ways they were a tribe apart in Uganda. The traditional teaching of the Karamajong was that God had created all the cattle in the whole world for them! It was their sacred duty to go and take back the cattle in anyone else's possession and restore them to their rightful owners – who were, of course, themselves. They had always had mixed success in this religious endeavour, because other tribes – mainly the neighbouring Teso and Acholi tribes – also had spears, clubs, bows and arrows, and brave young men in equal numbers to themselves. It was the AK47 that upset the traditional balance of power. We have to thank the Russian soldier General Mikhail Kalashnikov for his contribution to world terrorism!

In recent years their situation had worsened. The Karamajong population was increasing, but their cattle were lacking the pasture they needed to thrive. The rains had become unreliable and grazing was in short supply. They needed more cattle than their deteriorating land could support. The arrival of the guns changed everything. Now they could raid the peaceful Iteso with impunity. They just shot anyone who didn't flee fast enough from their raiding parties. They saw nothing wrong with this; they were, after all, just reclaiming what God had, in fact, already given to them. When the Ugandan People's Defence Force intervened and traced the cattle to Karamoja, they forcibly returned some of the cattle to their owners. The reaction of the Karamajong was loud weeping and wailing at the injustice of it all! In 2007, the Ugandan government embarked on a campaign to disarm the Karamajong. Wherever there was resistance the army took decisive and sometimes brutal action to achieve this. The loss of life and resulting suffering was great. However, if you point this out to most Ugandans, they have little sympathy for the Karamajong. They understandably think they deserve what they get! Even Christians only agree with some reluctance that God loves even the Karamajong. The rest of Uganda regards them as primitive and resistant to modernisation. They insisted on walking around virtually naked and regard it as dishonouring their traditions to wear clothes.

This was an early example of what some commentators are calling "Eco-wars". Increasing population in sub-Saharan Africa is causing a struggle for the limited water and grazing as the climate changes and the dry arid area of North Africa encroaches southward. The horrors of Darfur, where African villagers are being subjected to "Ethnic Cleansing" by armed Arabs who want more grazing, are the latest example.

One of the results of all this was that the young men of Teso found it increasingly difficult to come up with the right amount of cattle for a dowry when they wanted to marry. John was not immune to this problem. Beatrice being such an intelligent, attractive and well-educated young Christian woman with a good job meant that in normal circumstances her father could have expected a lot of cows as a dowry in the traditional Iteso way. But John didn't have any cows, he wasn't even a farmer, neither did he have much money – a teacher's pay is relatively poor. The tribal customs were going to need adapting to the new situation if John and Beatrice were to be married. The cows not taken by the Karamojong had been eaten by the LRA insurgents. After Museveni came to power there was even another internal insurgency by supporters of the former President Obote in an attempt to reinstate him. They also stole any cows they could find for feeding their fighters. By the time John and Beatrice wanted to marry, cows were a rare luxury.

Everyone realised that Beatrice's family was wealthier than John's. Simon Peter had made some money in his business ventures, but the cattle that were the traditional wealth of the Otuboi village community had largely gone. John had a business mind and he had done a little business with Simon Peter, who was by now, one of the town's councillors, so they were not strangers. Simon Peter had at various times written letters for John, giving him permission to sell goods in other parts of the region. Letters from a council member were necessary to prove you were an honest trader and not selling stolen or smuggled goods. President Museveni came to power on 29th January 1986. Uganda's best leader in modern times, he has brought relative stability and economic growth to a country that has endured decades of government mismanagement, rebel activity and civil war.

Very importantly, Simon Peter knew that John was a good man. He could see that he was an honest, hard-working Christian, who would care for his firstborn daughter. This was reassuring for him, but on the negative side his friends and relatives came round with their own advice. They informed him that John's family were poor, they had lost all their cattle, so he wouldn't get much for his daughter's dowry. Simon Peter began to waver and wonder if he could find a more suitable match for Beatrice. Beatrice is nothing if not strong minded. She informed her father that she had made her own decision. Perhaps, in the back of her mind were the painful memories of having to become a proxy mother to four younger siblings at the tender age of ten, a reminder that part of her childhood was snatched away. She was not about to lose control of her life again. Saying no to John was not an option that she was prepared to accept.

It was about this time that John met Donald Hemmingway, the retired Pentecostal Pastor from New Zealand, who was visiting the area. Donald was a friend of John's father, and John was helping his father make the arrangements for Donald's visits. John's father was already a pastor and led a group of churches further north in the Teso region, around their ancestral village of Otuboi. These were the churches that Donald was visiting and helping in various ways, including teaching and training leaders. John was his main interpreter for the meetings. He soon noticed John's leadership abilities and saw enormous potential in him. He asked John's father if he would release John to go to Bible College, offering to raise the sponsorship for his fees and expenses. John's father agreed. He also saw his son's potential and the offer of sponsorship was a wonderful opportunity. When Donald put the idea to John, he also accepted. John explained to Donald that he was engaged to be married. So the idea was put on hold while the marriage was arranged and celebrated. After that he could think about going to Bible College.

The traditional negotiations over the dowry were difficult. In the absence of any cows, an equivalent sum of money was decided on – one point three million Ugandan Shillings (£367). This was no solution because the village communities simply didn't have any money in their lives; their whole economy was based on cows. The economy of most villages like Otuboi had been destroyed and it would take years to recover. It was a dilemma because the idea of taking a bride – especially one as desirable as Beatrice – without any dowry was so against centuries of culture, it was unthinkable.

John was not afraid of hard work. He prepared a one acre field and planted it with potatoes. When they were harvested, he took them to the capital city, Kampala and sold them for 250,000 Shillings. Once the transport costs had been paid, this left only 200,000. John paid what he had. It wasn't much, but at least the dowry tradition had been honoured and something was paid for the bride.

John and Beatrice married in 1991. After the wedding they lived in accommodation that was given for the use of teachers at the school where John taught. About ten months later, their first son was born and naturally they called him Donald. When the child was three months old, Donald Hemmingway asked John if he was now ready for Bible College and he confirmed that he was ready to go. It was big step to leave his wife and child and go to Kaniki Bible College in Zambia, but it was a great opportunity to be trained for the ministry. As John's own Christian faith had grown, he had an increasing desire to be a pastor. Without Donald's help, training would not have been possible.

Before leaving, he moved Beatrice and the baby to a two-roomed rented house. A young girl moved in to care for the baby while Beatrice continued her work as a teacher. Immediately John had left, Beatrice and the baby came under spiritual attack. The baby was continually sick with one illness after another. The child even lost consciousness with a malaria induced coma, and Beatrice realised he was dying. She went to ask help from her neighbours. It was night and no one would open the door to her. This was because at that time it was the height of a local insurgency against the government and night time was the most dangerous. People were wondering if the fighting might come into the town at that time. All she could do was go back and cry out to God for the life of her firstborn. After an hour, Donald opened his eyes and the fever began to recede a little. This doesn't normally happen. For Beatrice, this was a significant miracle; her baby was back from the dead.

The next morning she took the baby to the clinic for some treatment. Later in the day a cousin of John's visited her. She was feeling very alone and vulnerable and was afraid that the fever would return that night – as fever so often does in children. She asked the man to accompany her to her father's house. They went on his bicycle (three on a bicycle is nothing unusual in Africa). As they arrived at Simon Peter's house, John's cousin began ringing his bicycle bell. Her grandfather was visiting at the time and had heard that the baby was sick again. Hearing the bell, he looked out of the window and saw the baby in Beatrice arms. He panicked and came rushing out thinking the baby had died. The death of sick babies is very common in Africa. They were almost expecting that this baby, who was suffering repeated illnesses, would die. Simon Peter advised her that she must not stay alone. She stayed in her father's home that night and the cousin returned to stay in Beatrice's house to keep an eye on her few possessions.

It is very difficult for parents of young babies to know if their illness is malaria, and many children die because of this. Children rarely recover naturally from malaria. They are either given appropriate treatment or they die in a week or less. It is the biggest killer in Africa. The malaria bearing mosquito is the second most dangerous creature on the planet (mankind being the most dangerous – only we kill our own kind!).

Through phone calls and letters John was aware of his child's continual sickness and he too was worried that the baby would die. He had been sharing the situation with the staff and students of Kaniki Bible College for prayer and support. One day Peter Pedersen called John into the office to discuss the situation. He told John that Beatrice and the baby needed to join him at the college. He would find some sponsorship and asked Donald to help with travelling costs and expenses.

Eventually it was agreed that Kaniki would sponsor Beatrice's fees at the college and Donald Hemmingway would raise the other living costs and the transport cost for Beatrice and the baby to come to Kaniki. As it would be cheaper to travel by bus than to fly, this was the route that they would take. Everyone was excited at the prospect. Beatrice had no experience of international travel and the thought of it made her nervous. She was now twenty-two years old. Unfortunately, no one realised just how difficult and dangerous it would be for a young woman with a small baby to travel the 5,000 kilometres south from Soroti to Ndola by public transport. The journey was to be the most difficult thing she had ever done; but God was with her.

CHAPTER 5

Evil Descending

Born in 1962 in a village near Gulu in Acholiland, Joseph Kony was twenty-five years old when he took on the family mantle of evil. Through various ceremonies and blood covenants at the traditional witchcraft sites in the Acholi district – the most northern in Uganda – and bordering the Sudan, he gave himself to the same religious spirits that had possessed Severino Lukoya and Alice Auma. The covenant that he cut with Satan was the same as all such deals – power in exchange for blood, death and destruction. Power is gained through worshipping the spirits and it is exercised through acts of evil.

He first communed with the spirits and then began to gather elements of the previous movement around him. He called his group "The Lord's Resistance Army" (LRA). The spirits presented him as a "Christ" figure who would save his people. Thus he completed an unholy trinity formed by himself, Severino Lukoya and Alice Auma – a false father, false spirit and an antichrist. The constant theme of them all was a pseudo-religious cult. Kony had to be persuaded by some of his more experienced commanders that attacking in the formation of a cross was not a good idea from a military perspective, even if it did enhance the religious aspects of the cult.

They were a group of thugs who were able to buy guns across the border in Sudan. Southern Sudan was embroiled in civil war at the time and the gun runners of the world made sure there was an ample supply for anyone with a few dollars to spend. Millions of AK47 assault rifles from the former Communist Eastern block are available in the trouble spots of the world. The AK47 with its familiar curved thirty-round magazine was cheap, robust, readily available and reliable.

It was clear to Kony that if he was going to make an impact on the area and deliver his side of the deal, he would need a lot more soldiers than the rag tag bunch of drunken thugs he commanded. If sufficient adults wouldn't join him, he decided that he would use children. Children don't need to be persuaded, they can be abducted and forced through violence, fear, drugs and brainwashing to become soldiers. Any child big enough to carry a gun could be used. Children aged from about ten to twelve were the targets. Kony began raiding Acholi villages. Anyone not quick enough to escape was captured. Many of the adults were tortured and killed. Women were raped and then either killed or mutilated. Large numbers of the rural population became *Night Commuters*. Before dark they left their villages and walked into the nearest town for the night. LRA attacks on villages were usually at night and the towns were a much safer place to be. Local government and NGOs did their best to give people a place to sleep. They slept in schools and church halls, with relatives, or just on the streets.

One NGO had built an agricultural training school in Soroti. For two years after its construction it was used to accommodate about two hundred children from local villages at night. Large areas became depopulated as the people fled south and were relocated as "Internally Displaced People" (IDPs) in makeshift camps that soon deteriorated into squalid, unhealthy shanty towns. The Ugandan People's Defence Force patrols driving north reported thousands of dead bodies, many lying at the roadside. Local services completely broke down in the affected areas. Schools, shops, businesses, agriculture and transport ceased to function. At the height of the insurgency, eighty-five percent of the people of the northern regions were displaced as they fled the LRA. Most of them went to the decrepit IDP camps.

The catalogue of murder, torture and mutilation is long and gruesome and no attempt will be made here to describe it in greater detail. However, it is important that we realise the typical nature of the evil that possessed these men. Common mutilations were the cutting off of limbs, cutting off lips, noses and ears, leaving the women and children horribly disfigured for life and unable to marry. Sometimes breasts were cut off, often leading to death through blood loss or infection – a slow painful death. Babies were cut from their mothers' wombs and killed. Many were burned to death as their villages were set on fire. Countless others were just slashed, eyes gouged out, some were stabbed or clubbed to death – bullets cost money and were to be kept in reserve for real fighting. The aim of the mutilations was to intimidate and terrify the wider population of Acholi district and beyond. No evil was too extreme for these men and the spirits that controlled them. Spirits can only control a person in this way if there is the willing participation of the human agent. Every person has a free will from God. There is no excuse or mitigation for such horrors.

This cannot be said of the innocent children. From the beginning, the signature tactic of the LRA was the abduction of children. Boys and girls were rounded up in each village and forcibly taken into the bush. They were forced to march long distances through the night, back to the LRA bases. Anyone who couldn't keep up was killed. Once back at base, the "training" began. The girls were immediately given to the LRA commanders as sex slaves and domestic servants. Kony had fifty-four wives and an uncounted number of children. If a boy had been abducted at the age of ten or twelve, by the time he was sixteen or seventeen he could be a commander. Such was the age range of this "army". Only the most senior commanders were mature adults and they controlled everything. The children were often used as human mules to carry heavy weights over long distances. Anyone who couldn't manage the work was beaten or killed. Any girl who resisted rape in any way was simply killed as a lesson to the other girls. Many of them became mothers by the age of twelve or thirteen. Estimates of the number of children abducted range from twenty to thirty thousand. About half have never been seen again. Exact figures have been impossible to calculate.

Bad as this treatment was, it was nowhere near the worst thing that happened to these children. They had to be turned into brutal killing machines. This was accomplished through a variety of methods. They were first beaten and brutalised themselves. Then they were forced to beat and kill other children. The simple means of coercion was – beat or you will be beaten. Torture and kill or worse will happen to you if you refuse. *You do it to him or her, or it will be done worse to you.* Under the influence of drugs, demons and alcohol, the unimaginable became frequent. Then there was the indoctrination. Older commanders would give long speeches to the children about how evil their parents were. It was their duty to kill their parents, aunts and uncles. Loyalty was only to be to the LRA and their commanders. It was their religious duty to God to obey their commanders. Any loyalty to family would be punished, often with death. There are a number of recorded incidents of children killing their parents or other family members. The way to advance themselves in the organisation and to better their living conditions was by demonstrating loyalty. This was achieved through brutality. The more brutal a child became, the more loyal that child was considered to be. These young children lived in a dark, surreal world of evil, violence, fear, drugs, cannibalism and witchcraft.

Uganda has a long history of inter-tribal conflict, often with a political or religious badge attached to it. Shocking as this violence was, Ugandans were further appalled because this was Acholis attacking and abducting their fellow tribal members. It seemed that the traditional and all-powerful tribal allegiance meant nothing! The advance of the LRA eventually engulfed the entire Acholi region, but Teso was not spared in any way. About half the children abducted were from the Teso region.

Children were relatively easy to deal with once they had been caught. The problem was in catching them. They tended to run away rather quickly into the bush as soon as they heard any trouble in their village – usually in the middle of the night. This led to attacks on or near to schools. Grabbing children as they left school had to be attempted in daylight and many children were taken in this way. A more effective strategy was attacking boarding schools during the night. The schools were, by nature of their design, walled and the opportunity for escape limited. Many of the boarding schools were run by the Catholic Church and provided an excellent education for the children. Places at the schools are highly valued by the parents who have funds for the reasonable fees.

Among the schools attacked were the Sacred Heart School from where between June 1987 and March 1998, a total of 138 cases of abduction were recorded; Sir Samuel Baker School, from where on 21st August 1996, 39 students were abducted from their dormitory; and St. Mary's College, Lacor from where 32 girls were abducted on 20th August 1992 and another 23 girls taken on 23rd July 1996. Primary Schools recorded as many as 3,384 known abductions. Total cases of known abductions of school children, however, stands at 5,545 in this district alone, but it is likely to be higher than this. Evil has no mercy on children and makes no allowances for their tender years. Their innocence is of no consequence. Only their suffering and early death is the aim of Satan and his army of destructive spirits.

The Aboke Girls

The most fully documented of all the school abductions was St. Mary's College for girls in Aboke, situated in northern Apac District. It is one of the best schools in northern Uganda and has a high academic reputation. Students are not required to be Catholic to attend the school. The students were girls from many backgrounds aged thirteen to sixteen. Most LRA activities at this time were concentrated within the three districts in Acholiland comprising Gulu, Pader and Kitgum. However, the violence sometimes reached into the bordering district of Apac. By the middle of 1996 the security situation in the district had again worsened. The rebels had already abducted ten schoolgirls, seminarians and villagers, as well as killing others whom they had run across as they marched. The soldiers of the UPDF had been replaced by Local Defense Unit (LDU) militia.

Rumours began to circulate through the countryside that the LRA was beginning to look at St. Mary's College as a likely target. Consequently, in September 1996, the LDU militia stated that they must move the students and staff from the college sixteen kilometres away to the town of Ikeme. Sister Alba, the Mother Superior, was naturally very reluctant to do so unless it was absolutely necessary. She sent Sister Rachele Facera (both were Italian missionaries) to negotiate with the LDU commanding officer, who agreed to set up a night patrol on condition that the school could provide a pickup truck to transport the soldiers to the college at night and back to Ikeme at dawn. The LRA almost always attacked at night so this was a key breakthrough. Nineteen soldiers were assigned to the protection of the college, but Sister Alba, feeling that this level of militia presence was insufficient to stop an attack, sent Sister Rachele Facera by bike to ask again for fifty soldiers, stating that she would otherwise close the school. Sister Rachele did not have a way to transport the soldiers she was requesting, and the LDU officer placated her by saying that he would know if the situation became dangerous and would then immediately send word to them to evacuate the school.

By October 9th the soldiers had not yet arrived at the school. This was an annual holiday to celebrate Ugandan Independence. The staff of the school always made sure that the girls enjoyed this day with traditional dancing and a generous supply of sweets, fizzy drinks and other goodies. The store room held these supplies for the evening party. However, something was wrong today and the girls could sense it. The three Italian sisters who managed the school did their best to act normally, but they knew that danger was near and the next day they would have to move the girls if the soldiers didn't come to protect them.

The three Sisters held a meeting to decide on a plan of action. The option of moving the girls out of the school and dispersing them was discussed, but it was already dark and the possibility that LRA rebels would be waiting outside to attack deterred the sisters from this course. An hour later the girls were sent to bed early, though the Mother Superior stayed up until 11:30pm to pray in the chapel. The girls went to their dormitories and locked themselves in. They all knelt on that hard floor and prayed before going to sleep.

At 2:30 am, the night watchman at the college knocked on Sister Rachele's door with a note of fear in his voice, "Sister, the rebels are here!"

Sister Rachele immediately woke Sister Alba and then moved out of the convent towards the front gate of the compound (which was actually just a net) and spotted the rebels outside the gate. Thinking that the rebels had been slowed by the gate and that they may be able to evacuate the girls through the back gate, the Nuns moved back towards the four dormitories, each of which had about fifty students. However, as they drew closer they saw flashlights around the dormitories and realized that the LRA had already come in through the back gate. In the knowledge that, if caught, the rebels would force them to open the doors, Sisters Alba and Rachele woke the one older nun, Sister Matilde, and together hid in the compound's stock house. Through the night they heard the sounds of rebels moving through the compound but never the voice of any of the girls, giving them hope that the rebels had been kept out of the dorms by the reinforced iron doors and windows. Later estimates put the number of armed rebels at about two hundred. They burned the school vehicle, ransacked the clinic and unsuccessfully attempted to burn several other buildings. The rebels actually gained access to the dormitories by breaking through the brickwork around the windows. They warned the girls that anyone who made a noise or cried out would be killed. The girls were intimidated into silence or quietly wept. Needless to say, they were stricken with fear.

The sisters lay hidden listening to the banging as the rebels attacked the walls of the hostels. As dawn approached, the nuns heard the sounds of the rebels leaving. They were convinced that they had left without any of the girls. Surely they would hear the girls crying or calling out. At first light (approximately 6:30am) Sister Alba noticed a small group of girls wandering in the open. When asked if they were okay, Claudia, a girl in the second year class, told them that the other girls had been taken away. The sisters rushed to the dormitories for classes four, five and six, but the girls who were inside, believing that the rebels had captured the nuns, refused to open the doors to them. Eventually the students were persuaded to come out. They reported to the sisters that the rebels had abducted dormitories one, two and three. In the confusion it was not possible to accurately count how many had been taken. They estimated that it must be about one hundred and fifty. They had hoped that the rebels had gone away having just stolen the stores of food and any valuables that they could find. To their horror, their worst fears had been realised. To add to their anguish, they knew that they had been taken by men who had a fearsome reputation for cruelty, barbarism and cold blooded murder.

The girls had been ordered by the commanders to dress in dark clothes, preferably ones that would protect them from the bush. They put their school uniforms on. Then they were lined up and their hands tied behind their backs and then tied to each other in groups of five or six. Anyone who talked was beaten. They were marched off in one long line at a brisk pace through the enveloping bush. It was a cold morning and it had been raining. They tramped through the mud, gripped by fear. Silent tears streaked down their faces as they stumbled along, wondering what was going to become of them. Many prayed to the God of the white nuns to help them.

One of the girls, Ellen, asked a soldier where they were going. He just told her to be brave. Strangely, there was a note of sympathy in his voice. She turned to look at him. She was shocked to see that this "soldier" carrying his gun looked younger that she was. In fact most of them were the same age as the girls or younger. Ellen realised that he too had been abducted and marched through the bush, suffering the same fear that she now felt. She could even feel sorry for him and his parents. Only the commanders were older. Not far from the school they halted while the commander inspected the girls. Some were judged to be too small for the heavy work and marching that the rebels knew lay ahead of them. These were separated and sent back. After the march resumed, shots were fired from their right. Everyone dived to the ground and the rebels fired back. In the confusion, a few girls freed themselves and escaped. This made the commanders very angry. As a punishment, the soldiers lined up in two ranks and the girls were made to run the gauntlet through the middle as the soldiers beat and kicked them.

Back at St. Mary's, Sister Rachele immediately volunteered to go after the girls and Sister Alba agreed. Sister Rachele changed clothes and took some money from the office to try to buy the girls' freedom. Sister Rachele had taught biology in the school for fourteen years. She was in her late forties but slim and fit. She could walk all day if required. Courageously, two of the male teachers, Bosco and Tom, also volunteered to accompany her in the pursuit. As Ugandan males, their going after the girls could be taken as a provocation by the rebels – they were almost certainly signing their own death warrants if they accompanied the nun. Sister Rachele agreed to take the younger of the two, Bosco. He said to Sister Rachele, "Come Sister, let us go and die for our girls."

They were about to leave when they were met by a thirteen year old student who had just been raped but left behind as she was unable to march because of her injuries. Leaving the child with Sister Alba, Sister Rachele and Bosco left the college at about 7am. The rebels had looted a large amount of candy and drinks that the college had bought for the Independence Day celebrations and the pursuers found that they could follow a trail of candy wrappers and drink bottles across the bush.

They eventually came across a man who was fleeing the LRA group and he was able to confirm that they had a group of girls with them. LRA bands were known to plant anti-personnel mines on their trail to discourage pursuit, so Bosco soon took the lead, telling Sister Rachele to only step into his footprints. If one of them was going to tread on a mine, it should be him. The courage of this young man was incredible. After wading through a swamp, Sister Rachele and Bosco were joined by a woman whose girl had also been abducted by the passing band. She joined them and hoped that maybe she could get her daughter back. Surely, even these evil men would have to respect the white sister, dressed in her white habit. She had God's authority, everyone knew that.

Shortly, as they crested a ridge, they saw a group of rebels ahead of them. They hurried on down the valley and soon the three emerged from some dense brush to find themselves facing the levelled rifles of thirty rebels arrayed in two lines, but no sign of the girls. Sister Rachele was depending on two factors: she was white and a foreign nun; she was also hoping for a miracle. The fact that she was white might lead the rebels to treat her with more caution than they would a Ugandan, and her status as a nun was a position that carried respect in a religious country; it might help her when dealing with a group that was led by a religious mystic such as Joseph Kony. Sister Rachele had spent a year and a half in Gulu and knew enough of the Acholi language to begin speaking with the man who identified himself as the leader of the LRA band. He was Mariano Ocaya, who, among a group known for their inhuman brutality, had the reputation of being more brutal than the rest.

Sister Rachele offered the money and asked for the girls' freedom. He informed her that he didn't want the money she had brought but, in response to her request that he release the girls, to her astonishment, he replied, "Do not worry. I will give you the girls."

The leader ordered the woman who had joined Bosco and Sister Rachele to leave. The LRA rebels then continued to march up the ridge. Sister Rachele stayed close to Ocaya in the knowledge that only he could release the girls. They caught up with the main group that held the girls and continued walking with the rebels and their exhausted prisoners. Looking at the group, Sister Rachele realised that others had been captured during the raids this group had carried out. Eventually the group made camp near the railroad at Acokara.

Commander Ocaya told Sister Rachele to separate the St. Mary's College girls from the other captives and warned her against trying to add any other captives from the group. Sister Rachele began to think that she would actually get all the girls back, but at that moment a

UPDF helicopter gunship passed overhead, forcing everyone to scatter and hide in the brush. Then Ocaya ordered everyone to resume marching again. Crossing the railroad tracks, the group came under fire from UPDF soldiers and everyone scrambled for cover. For four hours, the group continued on a forced march, periodically hiding from the gunship searching the area, as the column's rearguard slowed the UPDF soldiers. The group, eventually losing the UPDF, arrived in a camp where there were still more abductees. The St. Mary's College girls were again separated from the others. One of Ocaya's "wives" took Sister Rachele behind a hut to bathe, where they had an argument when Sister Rachele refused to change out of her habit into a dress. She knew that the religious clothing tended to have an inhibiting effect on the rebel commanders. When she returned, Bosco whispered to her that some of the girls were not being released. Sister Rachele asked Ocaya if he was releasing all the girls and he shook his head. He then wrote "139" in the dirt with a stick and next to it "109" and said that he was releasing 109 and keeping 30. He had selected them for "desirable traits" while Sister Rachele was absent. He selected the ones that looked the strongest and the most attractive.

When Sister Rachele protested, Ocaya said that she could write a letter to Joseph Kony with the names of the girls and he might agree to release them. Taking a piece of paper, Sister Rachele went back to the girls and saw the thirty that had already been separated. When she approached the thirty began calling out to her to save them. At an order from Ocaya, nearby soldiers began beating and kicking the girls. When they fell silent, Ocaya again ordered Sister Rachele to write down their names. As she came close, the girls again asked her to help:

"Sister, please don't leave us."

"Sister, will you return tonight?"

"Sister, will you bring the bed sheets tonight?"

"Sister, I am having my period, will you bring the toilet tissue tonight?"

"Sister, I am my mother's only daughter."

"Sister, they will rape us all tonight."

Every cry from her girls pierced her heart like a spear. Again, Sister Rachele asked Ocaya to release the remaining thirty also, but he replied that either thirty would stay or all would stay. One of the girls, Angela, offered to write the names because Sister Rachele's hand was shaking too much. Ocaya then insisted that she join him and the other LRA commanders for tea and cookies! In his twisted thinking, he imagined that sitting down with the white Nun in her white habit for a civilised snack with polite conversation would enhance his ego and reputation – that this little farce would somehow paint him as a reasonable and civilised person instead of the monster he actually was. It might even have impressed the men, but they would be the only audience that might appreciate this pantomime.

When she returned, Angela whispered that a girl called Janet had slipped into the 109. Sister Rachele knew that Ocaya was thoroughly capable of ordering all 139 to stay if he found her trying to sneak one of the thirty out, so he went to Janet and told her that she was endangering the entire group. Janet fell to her knees in tears and asked forgiveness and rejoined the thirty. After telling Judith, the head girl of the class, to look after the other 29, Sister Rachele and Bosco took the 109 and after a long and exhausting trek back through the bush, found their way back to St. Mary's college.

News of the abduction shocked the nation. Church groups began to meet to pray for the deliverance of the Aboke girls, their prayers sealed with bitter tears. Over the next few days, distraught parents came to the school to either collect their daughters or to face the overwhelming shock of seeing their daughter's name posted on the notice board as still missing. The loss of the thirty girls was not the end of the story. Through this horrendous situation, God, in His own economy in the heavenly realm, was about to accomplish something truly remarkable in spite of the tragedies that were about to unfold.

CHAPTER 6

Long Way Down

In March 1992 Beatrice began her epic journey by African bus. There are different classes of bus in Africa. Some are air-conditioned luxury monsters that roar through the villages eating up the miles in a great cloud of dust. Others are affectionately known as "Chicken buses". Beatrice took the cheaper option.

Donald Hemingway sent about one hundred dollars for the journey. The problem was that Beatrice didn't know what the various stages of the journey would cost. There was the bus fares, plus overnight stops in cheap hotels that might be needed, and of course she would need food. Baby Donald was seven months old, but he could survive on breast milk. It was all an unknown quantity and throughout the long journey there was the fear of not having enough money to complete it.

Loaded down with her suitcase in one hand, the baby, blanket and nappies in a bag in the other, they commenced the trip. Beatrice's father-in-law accompanied them on the first leg to the Kenyan border. This was in a "Mutatu" which is a minibus taxi, common all over Africa and many other parts of the world. These are always overcrowded and usually stiflingly hot. Not an easy place to sit with a baby in your arms, especially when he needs a nappy change!

They arrived at the border by early afternoon and Beatrice purchased a ticket for the overnight bus to Nairobi. The bus departed at seven in the evening and they managed some fitful sleep until it arrived at Kenya's throbbing capital city of three million souls. Tired and stiff, Beatrice alighted from the bus at one of Nairobi's loud and chaotic bus stations in the early morning before it was even daylight. She wondered where she could find her bus for the next leg of the journey, which was to Dar es Salaam, the coastal capital of Tanzania and largest port in East Africa. She waited until all the passengers were off her bus and asked the driver where she could catch the next bus.

To her dismay, he told her that it would go from another bus station, far from this one, on the other side of this vast city. Beatrice had never before been out of Uganda and didn't have any idea how to find her way around Nairobi. They even spoke a different language. Her communication would have to be with people who spoke the lingua franca of English. It seemed a naïve question to ask the driver, but she asked him if he could take her there. Africans usually try to help each other, especially if the other party is poor or in trouble. Looking at this young woman, seeing her baby and situation, the driver had compassion and said he would take her there. Instead of immediately taking his bus to the garage and going home for a well earned sleep, he drove across town to the bus station that Beatrice needed. Anyone who knows the eternal gridlock of central Nairobi traffic will realise what a sacrifice this kind man was making for Beatrice. God was with her.

The driver set her down at the bus station and said farewell. This bus station was almost deserted at this early hour. This was partly because most of the buses departed from this particular station much later in the day. In fact, her bus to Dar es Salaam was another overnight journey which meant she now had to wait the whole day. She had not yet had any breakfast and she was feeling hungry. As she sat there feeling lonely and vulnerable, two men approached her. She immediately felt a check in her spirit. She didn't like the look of them. They asked her if she was going to Tanzania and she told them she was. They urged her to go with them because they had a Mutatu and it needed three more passengers to fill it, then it would depart immediately. This is always the system with the Mutatu taxis. The drivers wait until their seats are all filled before they will begin the journey. Only this way can they make a living after they have paid the owner of the bus, the fuel and the many bribes imposed on them by corrupt police at the ubiquitous checkpoints. It would have been a better prospect than waiting all day if it were true. However, she didn't trust them, so ignored their supposed offer. She sat there feeling nervous; this bus station was not a safe place; these men were still hanging about.

After a short while a small group of people came and sat near her. She could overhear their conversation and they were talking about Jesus and things to do with their church. Realising that they were also believers, she introduced herself, explaining that she was also a believer. They told her that the two men were thieves and that she was right not to trust them. There were no Mutatus going to Tanzania, only the overnight buses. Meeting the group of Christians was a great comfort and encouragement to her – God was watching over her. They showed her which of the buses would be hers. It was parked with numerous others, all dark and silent at this early hour awaiting their time to depart in the afternoon or evening.

Several hours later, the owners of the bus arrived and she tried to board. The owners told her that the bus didn't go until seven in the evening and that she should find a hotel and rest until it was time. She explained that she didn't know any hotels and didn't have any spare money. Again African compassion was evident. They took her to a nearby inexpensive hotel and paid for a room and some food for her. She was able to eat a little, rest, have a shower and bathe the baby. She was afraid to sleep much in case she overslept and missed the bus. Restless, she returned to the bus station at three in the afternoon.

When it came time to board, an elderly fellow passenger helped her. He carried the baby and assisted in the boarding. All through the journey he was kind to her. He explained that he once went to Uganda to try to sell some goods and many Ugandans that he met were kind and helpful to him throughout his trip. He never forgot this, and realising she was a Ugandan he wanted to do everything he could to help. He was particularly helpful at the difficult Tanzanian border crossing. He cleared immigration and customs for himself while Beatrice waited in the bus. He then took her documents and luggage and cleared everything for her. This would have been a real trial with the baby in her arms.

The long journey to Dar es Salaam took until noon the next day. Beatrice's new friend explained that the train to Zambia went from the main station which was some distance from the bus station. He carried her luggage off the bus. Then he looked round and made a few enquiries until he found a group who were also going to Zambia. He asked them to help Beatrice get on the train. They allowed her to share their taxi to the station. When they arrived at the station, it was almost time for the train to depart. Her new friends already had their tickets, so they rushed to board.

Beatrice hauled her luggage and the baby to the ticket office, only to be told that the train was full. Her heart sank as she learned that the next train wasn't for another three days! She asked the ticket man what she should do for three days. He told her to find a hotel and stay there. She explained that she had no money for a hotel or food for three days. She pleaded with the man for any way to get on the train. He reluctantly told her that if she purchased a third class ticket she could board the train, but she wouldn't have a seat! She had no alternative but to pay for the ticket and haul everything aboard and locate herself in a corridor. She couldn't stay where she was, she was blocking the corridor, and people were continually walking up and down. After the train moved off at two in the afternoon, she looked in all the third class compartments for an empty seat, but every one was full. She found a washroom at the end of her carriage. She entered, closed the door and settled down, sitting on her luggage.

Through the afternoon, evening and the whole of the night, she stayed there. She breast-fed Donald, changed his nappies and tried to snatch a little sleep. This was by far the longest leg of the whole odyssey, more than 3,000 kilometres. The Tanzam Railway stretches from Dar es Salaam to Kapiri Mposhi in Zambia. The journey takes a minimum of two days. It was built in the 1970's by China, keen to pursue their campaign to win the allegiance of African nations for trade and political support. This small town on the Zambian Great North Road is not the place it was supposed to terminate. The original plan was for a coast to coast line. The line is slow and known for derailments and breakdowns with the trains generally arriving between eight and twenty-four hours late! The people who take this route are those who either have no alternative or enjoy the adventure! This particular train that Beatrice was on was not too bad. It broke down only once for a short time and needed some repair.

The cool African dawn arrived after the endless night in the washroom. The train stopped to let some passengers off and new ones on. Tired, hungry and stiff, Beatrice wondered if this was her chance to find a seat. Alas, all the third class seats were again filled. She asked the conductor for help. She had to lie down and get some rest. Seeing her distress, he ushered her into a second class compartment that had six bunks. The two at the top were taken by men, two in the middle by ladies and another lady in one of the bottom bunks, leaving one vacant. Beatrice occupied the bottom bunk because she had the baby. At last, a chance to sleep properly.

Baby Donald soon became the centre of entertainment for the others in the compartment so he was passed around and enjoyed getting to know some new friends. Beatrice heard that in second class they had a restaurant car. She was afraid that she wouldn't have enough money left for the onward journey, so she only purchased some tea. Having not had a drink since leaving the hotel in Dar es Salaam twenty-four hours previously she was very thirsty. She was also very hungry, but had no money to buy food and had not eaten since leaving Nairobi. Some of the ladies in her compartment had brought food with them. Seeing she was without food, they of course shared their pasta, chicken and drinking water with her – African hospitality culture demands this. The compartment was like one happy family sharing their stories and news. In the Western world, people can sit for hours with other passengers and never speak. Africans find this incomprehensible.

The last leg of this arduous journey from Kapiri Mposhi to Kaniki Bible College is only two hours drive. However, logistically, it is the most difficult. Beatrice had no idea how she was going to make it.

Kaniki is twelve miles east of Ndola town, near the Congo border. Beatrice discussed her apprehension with her fellow travellers and they said they would help her to find the best way when they arrived. Inevitably, the train was hours late arriving and, to make things worse, it was getting dark. No one likes travelling in the dark. Would there be transport at the station? Taxi drivers mostly go home in the evening.

When the train finally pulled slowly into the station and juddered to a halt, there was a mad scramble for the available Mutatus. Passengers were frantically unloading boxes and bags and hastily negotiating the price of transport to Ndola, a hundred kilometres away. Beatrice's travelling companions joined the rush and she was left to "Sort out my own mess." She gathered her things and the baby as best she could and struggled off the train, feeling very much the stranger in a strange land. Her father had advised her to always ask the help of a policeman, because they always speak some English. The local language in this part of Zambia is Bemba.

This was good advice because, as one travels in Africa, it is common at the numerous police checkpoints to be asked by the police if you would give a ride to someone. She spotted a policeman and asked for his help. He approached a couple who were busy loading their goods into the back of a single-cab pickup truck. He asked the woman to help, thinking naturally that she would be more sympathetic to a young woman with a baby. She adamantly refused to help, which is very unusual. The policeman persisted, but still she refused. He then approached the man and he agreed to take Beatrice to Ndola, against the wishes of his girlfriend, who was angry at being overruled.

There would have been room for Beatrice to sit in the front cab because there are three seats, but this lady insisted that Beatrice sit in the back among the boxes and in the open. It was the coldest time of the year in Zambia and night had descended; it became very cold. To add to the problem, Beatrice had no warm clothes; she was not expecting cold weather. Uganda is on the equator, but Zambia is much further south. She sat on a box in the back of the truck trying her best to keep the baby warm. Her thin clothing was little protection against the cold, made colder by the draught from the movement of the vehicle. She began to shiver violently. By the time they reached Ndola, she was seriously near to hypothermia. Why did this lady refuse to help? She may just have been very hard hearted, but in Africa, as in most of the world, there is sometimes a prejudice against foreigners.

On arriving in Ndola at about eight in the evening, Beatrice asked the couple if she could stay in the hotel where they would be staying. The unsympathetic lady in the vehicle told Beatrice that they had helped her enough and she should go now. However, the man, seeing how cold she and the baby were, told her now to come into the front of the vehicle and he would help her find accommodation when he had distributed the goods to various shops around the town. His girlfriend went alone into their hotel. This took a further two hours. The man informed Beatrice that he worked for an important businessman who was the former governor of Ndola and when the deliveries were complete, he would ask him to help her.

They finally arrived at the large house of the former governor and the driver explained Beatrice's situation and how much she had just suffered in the cold. The businessman stayed alone in the house with just a house boy to do the cooking and chores and the boy was serving his boss supper when they arrived. The former governor readily agreed to help Beatrice and invited her to stay in the house for the night. He asked her if she was hungry and she said she was, but most of all she needed hot tea because she was still very cold. This kind man gave her tea and supper and showed her to a nice large bedroom with an attached bathroom. That night Beatrice slept well, warm and fed, thanking God for His mercy in leading her thus far.

The next day, her first job was to use the bathroom to shower and bathe the baby. She also took the opportunity to wash some clothes and nappies. The former governor offered to take her to Kaniki if she could put some fuel into his vehicle. Everyone in Ndola seem to know of Kaniki Bible College and, in fact, Kaniki visitors arriving at Lusaka airport are often surprised to discover that the immigration officials know all about Kaniki.

Fuel in this part of Africa at that time was about half the cost of what it was in the West. However, the salaries of ordinary people were only five to ten percent of salaries in the West, making fuel extraordinarily expensive. Today, it is almost the same price as in the West, making the problem even worse. Beatrice had been conserving her dwindling money as best she could, not knowing what bus, taxi and train fares were going to be. Now she was confident that this was the final leg of the journey, she could use the little she had left for the fuel, so she gladly agreed, giving him her final twenty dollars.

As they drove towards the Mufulira district outside of the town, Beatrice spotted a minibus coming in the opposite direction which had the Kaniki Bible College logo on it. She told the man that if he could turn and chase the minibus, he could save himself the twenty-five mile round trip to Kaniki. He quickly turned and overtook the bus. He explained that he had one of their new students and asked if they would take her to Kaniki. The minibus was being driven by the Dean of Students of Kaniki Bible College, who of course was delighted to take her. She said her farewell and thanked the businessman for his kindness and transferred to the college minibus. She finally arrived at the college before lunch, ending her epic journey that had taken about five days, but had seemed much longer.

Her husband John was not there to greet her because the students were all away on their annual evangelistic outreach in nearby towns for another week. Peter Pedersen, the Principal of the college, and his wife, Clara Marie, were there to meet her for the first time, commencing a friendship that was to become a major blessing in her life for many years to come. She stayed for that week in the home of the Dean of Students and his family until the students returned. Then both John and Beatrice were transferred to the married students' accommodation.

Beatrice's brief but nasty experience of illwill towards her as a foreigner by the lady in the pickup truck was an exception to normal African culture, but it was not to be the last. Another, far more deadly example, from a most unexpected source, awaited her during her time in Zambia.

Survivors, Eyewitnesses and the Lives of Others

CHAPTER 7

Below are the stories of just a handful of those whose lives have been blighted by the LRA. Each of the brief accounts below deserves a much fuller telling of their stories. It was obvious during the interviews that it was not easy for people to talk about their suffering. The purpose is for these few to represent the many whose lives have been affected and often devastated by the conflicts that they have endured. Some of them escaped severe suffering and others did not. All of them testify to a solid faith in God that has survived and sometimes been enhanced by their bitter experiences. With most of them, the names have been changed or omitted in these short narratives, but these are first-hand eye witness accounts and testimonies. There are a variety of different circumstances, experience and suffering. They are the few that hopefully give some kind of a voice to the many.

John Onyaro

John Onyaro was interviewed six months after he fled his village with his wife and children, one of them a newborn baby. First of all, John thanks God for His protection and saving his life. He was in his village church when they had a prophecy telling them that the LRA were coming and they must flee. This was confirmed later by one of the Arrow Boys (a militia group who had fought against a previous government) who also warned them to flee south to Soroti. He says, "I thank God because he sustained my life and many others in the church."

John is an ordinary Iteso farmer living with his family in his ancestral village. Forewarned, John and many others in their village prepared for what they knew would be a hurried flight. When they judged that the time had come, they gathered as much as they and the older children could carry and left their home, not knowing when they would be able to return. Everyone was reluctant to leave because their crops were almost ready for harvesting. They knew that they were leaving behind their food for the next twelve months and their seed for next season's planting. They are subsistence farmers, relying on the annual rains and harvest time. Giving up the harvesting of their crops was almost unthinkable. They would only do this when death was the only alternative.

Some of their fellow villagers who were his friends and neighbours delayed their departure too long. The LRA contingent arrived during the night. Many were caught and brutally beaten to death with clubs, mainly to the back of their heads, until their skulls were completely smashed.

John and his family now live in an IDP camp in Soroti, barely surviving on the meagre rations that NGOs and the churches are able to provide. He stays in this camp even though a larger camp with 23,000 residents has been established nearer his village. He stays because he has heard that the other camp has had no deliveries of food. Local Pastors also try to help them, but they themselves are poor. The camp has no clean water, medicine or medical help of any kind.

Many of their village's children have died from measles and malaria, and increasingly now, malnutrition in the various IDP camps. When asked what would be the circumstances under which he would return to his village, he explains that the problem is still security. Only when he feels that there are government soldiers in the area of the village to protect them, would he go back and farm his land. All the huts in their village were destroyed. He and his neighbours would have to begin again. They have no food or seed for planting and they have no money to buy seed. They can only return with considerable help to re-enter their annual cycle of planting and harvesting their food. This is the reason that once established, refugee and IDP camps seem to be required for many years to come. So often in Africa, the winding up of refugee and IDP camps by governments has to be done forcibly. Life in the camp may be difficult and unhealthy, but being cast out of the camp and being told to return home may mean malnutrition leading to death from disease or starvation.

John insists that his faith in God is still strong even in his difficult circumstances, because God has been merciful to him and he has faith that God will bring him through this difficult time and restore him to the contented, happy village life he and his family previously enjoyed. Throughout the interview he repeated one sentence over and over, speaking not only for himself, but also for his fellow residents in the camps:

"Life is *so* hard."

Melisa Agweru

Melisa comes from Katakwe. She thanks God for saving her from what she thought was going to be a life-destroying experience. The LRA came to her village at night and she was captured. She was abducted with her children but, unusually, she was not beaten or raped. She was soon released. Even her children were saved from bad treatment. God protected her on the long journey to Soroti. When she arrived exhausted and hungry in Soroti, the local church helped with food and a shelter.

She was delivered unharmed. She attributes this very unusual escape only to the mercy of God.

Margaret Apeney

Margaret comes from Katakwe and she is an active member of her church. When the LRA attacked her village her five children were abducted. She was devastated and cried out to God through bitter tears for their deliverance. At the time of her interview, two of her children had been rescued by the army. She is praying for the others. She joined the procession of refugees walking south to Soroti. On her arrival, the local churches helped her with food and getting her settled into one of the camps. It is usually the churches that quietly go about their ministry of mercy, filling in as many of the gaps left by the NGOs and the government as they can.

Mary

Mary was in her hut when the LRA attacked at night. Gunshots, shouting and screams suddenly shattered the still night air. She was too terrified to move and just huddled on the floor of her hut and hoped that no one would come in. She could hear that her neighbours' homes were being set on fire. Inevitably her hut was also torched. The fire spread with alarming speed and she realised that she was trapped. Her choice was clear. She would either die or brave the flames and get out. She did get out but with severe burns to about a third of her body. Hidden by the smoke, she ran for her life hardly noticing her injuries. Once she was clear of the village, the unbearable pain set in. She knew that she was in a bad way, but had no choice but to head south for Soroti in the darkness. After many agonising hours, she eventually staggered into Soroti and was admitted to hospital. She spent four months in hospital. Badly scarred, she is still in a lot of pain, but thanking God that her life was spared.

Christine Abuta

Christine is one of the executives of the widows' savings and loan association. Her husband died in 1988 in hospital and was buried in town. She had been cut off in her village by the rebels and was not able to take her husband's body home to be buried in his ancestral village. Not to be able to bury her husband in his ancestral family plot was a cause of great sorrow and cultural trauma for her. Eventually, after much suffering, she was able to escape and travel to Soroti.

She was jobless and sleeping on the streets or under trees. One day God gave her a vision in which she secured a fine job, but one that she had not even applied for. She rejoiced in the vision and shared it with her church. A couple of weeks later she was at a political rally in Soroti attended by the President. She was at the front of the welcoming crowd and to her astonishment, the President walked up to where she stood and asked if she had a job? She said that she hadn't and he then asked her if she would be his housekeeper in the Soroti Presidential Lodge.

Because she was already in the widows' savings group Beatrice suggested that she become their liaison with the government because she was already working for them. Christine had been surviving by purchasing bales of used clothing and selling them. She is making enough money now to begin thinking of a house for herself. She has already made enough to purchase the plot. Christine is an intelligent and enterprising widow who just needed the opportunity and encouragement to apply her talents to starting over again. God gave her that opportunity and she grasped it with both hands; not just for her own benefit, but also to help her fellow widows.

Florence

Florence is the Treasurer of the Teso widows' cooperative. Her husband died in 1995. He had a good job working at the Soroti flying school as an accountant. They lived in a government supplied house in town and saved part of his salary each month hoping to eventually build their own house. He died in hospital after a short illness and she took his body back to his village where she stayed for three days. A group of her husband's relatives came and killed their goats and took them to eat or sell. It was useless to protest, it was the custom. Then, while she was in the village, other relatives also came with a paper from the High Court and took it to the bank and withdrew all their savings which was a large sum of money. It was the money which she hoped would have been enough to build a small house. They had already purchased a plot. She only discovered the theft when she returned from the village. Again, it was useless to protest. A widow has no rights. Some of the governments in Africa, including Uganda, have outlawed this oppressive custom and are beginning to observe rights for widows. Unfortunately the law is often not observed.

She went to see her husband's colleagues at the flying school and told them what had happened. They were sympathetic and they raised some money for her and her seven children so that they could at least eat for a while. Then God opened another way for her. She has joined the widows association and has been able to survive by opening a small business. She has one child in university and all the others are at school. So far she has managed to pay the school fees, but it is a struggle. With a chuckle, she will often say, "My husband was an accountant and now I am a treasurer."

Violet

Violet's husband worked for the municipal council for ten years, a secure and reasonably paid job. He died in 2002 after a long battle with AIDS. They had been married for ten years and they had five children. Her husband had saved a lot of money and their future seemed secure. Once he became ill with AIDS symptoms, he used all the savings to pay for treatment and hospital bills. He was bedridden at home for his final two years. It was very difficult for the family, especially the children, to watch their father dying a slow and painful death. When the oldest needed to go to High School there was no money for fees. Violet kept begging for small loans from friends and family to meet the fees. She was a school teacher and so she could pay them back when her salary came. The salary was very stretched to pay the normal expenses and also the loans.

Her husband's older brother also lived with them and he had no job. She was able to get small loans from the bank but at an interest rate of 50%! She opened a small kiosk to sell things but never had enough stock to make progress. Now she is in the widow's association. This has helped her in two ways. She is now a born again Christian and that has changed everything. She can now get loans from the widows' savings and loan scheme for her business at a much more reasonable rate and now has a more secure future.

Pauline

Pauline and her husband fled their village because the LRA were in the area attacking villages. They were resettled in a camp, but there was a shortage of food there. They knew there was food in their village and the fields around it and they thought it was worth the risk to try to go and retrieve some. They had no trouble getting to their village and finding the food that was stored there, so they became optimistic that their expedition was going to be a success. Things went wrong while they were returning to the camp. They didn't know that the LRA were hiding in the roadside bushes ambushing people who passed.

Suddenly they found themselves surrounded by LRA thugs with guns. They grabbed the bicycle from her husband which was carrying the sacks of grain. She also carried food on her head. They instinctively looked around to see if there was any place to run. The ambush spot had been carefully chosen. Recent rains had left the low lying fields on either side of the road flooded and there was nowhere to run. Her husband looked at her and said, "Mummy, I am dead – this is my day. If you survive, please care for our children. Please keep them in unity with each other."

Pauline just stayed quiet, not wanting to admit that her husband's assessment was true. Again he said, "This is the day God has appointed for me to die."

The rebels were quiet, but still pointing guns at them. They surrounded her husband and began beating him with their rifle butts. Some of the soldiers came to her and took the food she was carrying and began beating her too until she collapsed. She was praying to God for deliverance as they beat her. The soldiers stopped beating her husband because he looked as if he was dead. Their leader asked the others if he really was dead. To make sure, he came with a heavy tree branch and hit his head with it, attempting to crush his skull. Then he came to her and told her to get up. A discussion began between the soldiers as to what they should do with her. One said, "Let us kill her too."

"No, let her go now," another said.

"Let's take her with us," said a third.

Eventually they took her with them and walked for about one kilometre until they came to their main group where their officer was. Pauline was praying and wondering what they were going to use to kill her. Then the officer came over with a thick stick and began beating her. He beat her on every part of her body except her head. Several soldiers then beat her and when the rod shredded, they fetched another and continued the beating. The soldier that had killed her husband brought a larger branch and hit her with it and she collapsed unconscious. They left her for dead and moved on.

When she recovered consciousness, she looked around and no one was there. She waited until she had recovered enough to stand up and staggered back to her husband. It looked like his life had returned to him. He was trying to get up in spite of being very near to death. She tried to bend to help him, but because her body was so beaten and swollen, she couldn't bend. Unable to help him, she hurried as best she could back to the camp, each step wracking her body with pain. Hardly conscious, she staggered into the camp and asked the soldiers to go and help her husband. She hoped that if they brought him back to the camp, he might recover. She collapsed again and was unable to speak as she went into deep shock. They took her to the clinic in the camp.

She was able to speak after a while and told them what had happened. No one would go for her husband without transport and there was none. The camp was guarded mainly by local militia boys, but only about ten remained there. The rest were out pursuing the rebels as they retreated north into Acholiland. Her husband lay on the road until another group of rebels passed by and saw that he was still alive. They made sure he was dead this time by beating his skull until it was crushed.

Her husband lay dead on the road for two days before he could be buried. It was months before Pauline recovered from her injuries.

Janice

Janice tells how the Karamajong killed her husband. They were in the safety of the refugee camp because of the LRA insurgency. He had a small business making saucepans which he sold at the local markets. From this business he was able to save enough to think about expanding it into a more profitable one. He joined a group that were taking cows to be sold at the market further south where it was safer. He even hoped to buy some for ploughing a plot of land.

On their return they were ambushed by the Karamajong who shot at the vehicle. He tried to jump from the vehicle and escape. He knew that the Karamajong were in the habit of simply killing everyone they robbed. As he landed on the road, the vehicle tyres were shot out and this caused the vehicle to swerve. Now, out of control, the vehicle swerved and knocked him down, then ran over him. He died on the spot.

There were UPDF soldiers nearby and, hearing the shots, they came and chased the Karamajong away. The bandits didn't get any cows but her husband had died in the attack. He was the only one to die. The vehicle and the Karamajong all fled the site leaving her husband lying dead on the road. Another vehicle returning to the camp came that way stopped when its occupants saw the body and recognised him. One person in the group had a cell phone who rang the camp with the bad news. The caller told the camp officer to go and tell Janice that her husband was dead. However, the officer didn't dare tell her. He just told others in the camp. No one wanted to tell her and by late afternoon, she was the only person in the camp who didn't know her husband was dead. Eventually a woman in the camp came to her and spoke her husband's name and asked if this was her husband. It was her son who responded to the question and said, "That is my daddy's name."

The woman now turned to the child and said, "Your daddy is dead."

The children began to cry but Janice didn't believe it. She thought that maybe he had just been injured. But others now came to her and told her to take heart and trust in God. She began praying, "God, please give me strength; I didn't think you would take away my husband while I am still so young."

Agnes Mahoka, one of the widows' leaders

New Life and Near Death

CHAPTER 8

When married students applied to Kaniki they were requested to try and avoid becoming pregnant while at college. The simple reason for this is that it seriously disrupts the mother's ability to study, sit exams and take part in the outreach programme. The couples are given family planning assistance to help them. Beatrice received this help, but accidentally became pregnant.

When the delivery time came and Beatrice went into labour, John called Birthe, a Danish doctor who worked at the college. She came with the necessary supplies and equipment ready to deliver the baby. Unfortunately, when she examined Beatrice, she realised that the baby was in a breech position. The doctor explained the complication to John and Beatrice and said she would need to go to the general hospital in town for the delivery. Birthe drove Beatrice to Ndola General Hospital. This was a painful ride, with extra strong labour pains because of the complication, over the fifteen kilometres of the bumpy Mufalira road.

On arriving at the hospital, she was taken up to the delivery ward. Birthe explained to the doctor and nurses that it was a breech birth and advised them on what they needed to do to facilitate the birth. The nurses immediately resented the situation and disagreed with Birthe as to the required procedure.

Why has this foreign doctor brought this problem to us? Why is she not finishing what she started? Why didn't she bring this patient to us in the first place? This patient is not even a Zambian. We want nothing to do with it.

Only on the orders of their own doctor did the nurses take any action, but with a very bad attitude. It was going to be necessary to cut Beatrice to open the way for the difficult delivery. Instead of doing this procedure in a careful and professional way, the nurse made a much bigger incision than was necessary in an angry reaction to being ordered by the doctor and resentment of the foreigners. The baby was delivered and it was healthy, but Beatrice wasn't. Birthe had waited in an adjacent room and when she heard that the baby had been delivered, she left to attend to the daily clinic she held at Kaniki. The hospital's doctor had also left the scene. It was eight in the morning.

Beatrice was now in a bad way. She held her healthy baby, but she was bleeding profusely and the bed was saturated with blood. She asked for a certain drug, which she knew from her first child's delivery was given to mothers who were bleeding after delivery. They said that they didn't have this drug in their hospital. Beatrice's head was spinning and she began to feel weak and disorientated because of the serious loss of blood. She was desperately thirsty and asked for a drink of water. The nurses asked her if she had any money, but she had no money with her, so they refused to give her the desperately needed drink.

The nurse who had made the incision began to realise the seriousness of the reckless action she had taken. Beatrice urgently needed to be stitched up or she would die from the blood loss. The other nurses now began to panic and distance themselves from this nurse. Their attitude was, *You caused this problem and you must sort it out.* This nurse said that she would get the doctor. But instead of doing this, she panicked, left the hospital and went home! No one had called the doctor. The other nurses now put the baby in a cot and fled the scene, leaving Beatrice and the baby alone while her very lifeblood ebbed away.

Hours passed as the life gradually leaked out of her body and no one came. Realising that she may well die in that hospital she cried out to God to help her. By three in the afternoon she was lying in a pool of her own blood. All through this time the baby was crying in the cot. She asked a passing nurse to bring her the baby. The nurse said, "How can I do that? You are lying in a pool of blood, where will I put the baby?"

Eventually, a doctor walked through her ward on his way to see a patient in the next ward. He glanced at her as he walked past and assumed that there was someone attending to her. As he returned, he saw that Beatrice was still there without anyone attending to her. Very unusually, this doctor was also a Ugandan who had worked for many years in Zambia. He greeted her in Bemba and she told him that she didn't speak Bemba.

"What language do you speak?" He asked.

"I speak English and Ateso." she replied.

Realising she was a fellow Ugandan, he became more concerned with her case. He asked the other nurses why no one was attending to her. They told him about the nurse who had made the mistake and how she had fled. They explained that it was not their duty to pick up the mistakes that she had made. Seeing the pool of blood and the weak, near-death state of Beatrice, he intervened and stitched her up himself before it was too late. He probably saved her life. God had other plans for Beatrice than dying in a hospital bed from wanton, criminal neglect. After the stitching, he ordered the nurses to attend to her. She was taken to the next ward and put in a clean bed and given a drink of water. She had not eaten or drunk anything since the previous day.

Beatrice was then told by the nurses to move to an ordinary ward. She was too weak to walk and was also in terrible pain. She asked the nurses for painkillers but they ignored her requests. They became very rude to her, telling her she must move to the other ward, but offered her no assistance. She just ignored them and lay waiting to see what would happen.

All this time, John was sitting in the waiting room downstairs, not knowing what was happening to his wife. He could have easily brought her a drink, but he knew nothing. Husbands were not allowed into the delivery wards of the hospital. He was finally told by the doctor that Beatrice had delivered the baby boy, but that he was still not allowed to visit until the evening. He went into town to see some friends and organised to bring in some food later. He finally saw Beatrice and the baby at seven in the evening.

When John came to the ward, Beatrice introduced him to the nurses, telling them that he was a Pastor. John's towering presence and the revelation that this was a man of God had a remarkable effect on the nurses. Now they became friendly and even brought her some painkillers. Beatrice couldn't help wondering what was wrong with these nurses that they couldn't bring her the Panadol before.

She stayed just that night in the hospital and the next day John came with friends from the church they were attending, who owned a car. They returned to Kaniki where both Beatrice and the baby could get proper care, good food and recover from her ordeal. A month later, she was able to resume her studies. They named the baby boy Prince Titus.

In the West we tend to take good health care for granted and we are appalled at such a story as this. This is a particularly bad example of the lack of professionalism, training and supervision that is so often seen in African government hospitals. Unfortunately, this is not an isolated incident. Many women giving birth have suffered from lack of hygiene and proper training in some African hospitals. This writer knows a young Zambian Pastor and his Mozambican wife who had an even worse experience a few years later than this incident.

Their first child, a baby boy, was born in another hospital close to the one where the previous incident took place. Incredibly, this very large hospital was without any water supply for about four years. The pumps bringing the water from the borehole had broken down and no one had repaired them. The hospital's director simply had to order his maintenance manager to carry out the repairs. The money for doing this just was not allocated. The tanks holding the remaining water on the roof began to leak and dirty brown water ran down the walls of the four storey building, including the walls of the wards. The Director's own office had dirty brown water leaking down the wall. Nurses and patients' relatives could be seen walking round the hospital carrying plastic containers of water brought from outside. It was all very unhygienic but water is obviously essential in any hospital and so it had to be brought in via plastic containers that may have once contained orange juice.

Our friend's baby was born normally, but through lack of basic hygiene and water, the cord was not cleaned properly. Consequently, when they returned home with the baby, an infection set in and the baby became feverish. They took the baby back to the hospital and he was admitted to a ward. It was a Friday afternoon and not much work was done at this time of the week, so no doctor came to see the baby that afternoon. Most of the doctors took off early for the weekend. They then discovered that in this hospital, no doctors worked over the weekend! If there was an emergency on a Saturday or Sunday it was just too bad. During this time the baby's fever worsened. Our friends sat watching and praying day and night. They hoped that a doctor would come on Monday morning when they returned from their weekend off. The doctors all came back, but every Monday morning is taken up by their weekly meeting! The baby died Monday lunch time. He was ten days old.

A couple of years after this sad incident, we were asked by local pastors to try to help the hospital. We applied to a British charity called Wilmslow Wells for Africa. It is based in the small Cheshire town of Wilmslow. They do a wonderful work of raising money all year round to fund wells in Africa. They have helped us many times to install boreholes to bring much needed clean water to African communities.

This was a more expensive project than they normally took on, but they agreed to see what they could do. Even though they raised the money, it still took two years to get the cold water supply restored. This was due to corruption and obstruction from various managers involved in the process. The temptation, where such incidents as described in this chapter happen, is to become angry, disillusioned and just give up. But to give up would be to concede defeat. As Christians we are in a spiritual war and we must never give up bringing the light of the Gospel of our Saviour Jesus Christ.

The Power of Forgiveness

CHAPTER 9

After an exhausting week of marching north east through the bush, the Aboke girls were brought to Kony's base in Southern Sudan where they were given to various commanders as "wives". We can only speculate that the Sudanese government's motive in hosting these monsters was to destabilise Uganda. Sudan has been attacking the population in the southern part of their country for over twenty years. The rest of Sudan is Arab, but the south is mostly African and Christian. Throughout these long years the Sudanese government has bombed innocent villages in the south in an attempt to subdue the population. Various Christian rebel groups have fought government troops and sometimes each other. As always, it tends to be the innocent civilians who suffer the most.

Sudan continues to prove itself to be a pariah nation. Having persecuted the Christian south for many years, they then allowed Osama Bin Laden to set up training bases in their country. They continue their attempts at ethnic cleansing by supplying arms, equipment, transport and encouraging the genocide of the population of Darfur, whose population are their own people politically and geographically, but also ethnically Africans. Outraged at the genocide in Southern Sudan, the Ugandan government protested loudly about the actions of the Sudanese government. This also gave them reason to support Kony and provide a safe haven for him and his followers.

Soon after arrival at the base, a girl named Jennifer went missing. When she was found hiding in a hut, the rebels dragged her into the open and ordered the others to beat her to death. The girls hit her lightly at first, but then the rebels surrounded the group and beat anyone who was not hitting Jennifer hard. Afterwards the LRA rebels left the corpse in the open and beat those who wept, both as an object lesson about attempting to escape and as a way to break the social ties between the girls.

Of all the horrors suffered by the Aboke girls, the death of Judith, the head girl, is notable for its brutality. It is Sister Rachele's belief that her request to Judith that she, "Look after the others" led her to do something that annoyed the rebels. One evening, Judith and another girl, Caterina, from a group of other captives, had their hands bound behind their backs and were attacked with sticks, bicycle chains and machetes. Caterina died of her wounds the following morning, but Judith was still alive 24 hours later and asked for water. The rebels instead dragged her into the forest and tied her to a tree. A group of captives gathering firewood found her body a week later. Her body had not started decomposing, indicating that she had not been dead for long.

Angelina Atyam was a midwife. She was particularly pleased when her daughter Charlotte passed the entrance exam and qualified to study at the famous St Mary's College for Girls, because it was her old school. She knew it had a good academic standard and good moral atmosphere in which her daughter could transit her adolescent years. She was nervous because of the rebels in the country and Charlotte also had her own fears. However, the chance to go to St. Mary's College for girls was such a great opportunity that she decided her daughter should go. She comforted Charlotte, telling her, "You must trust in God."

She prayed every day for her daughter and the safety of all at the school.

Early one morning while she was still asleep, her neighbour knocked loudly at her door. "Angelina, Angelina, the rebels have abducted the girls from St Mary's."

Angelina later said, "I screamed like a mad person."

She dressed and hurried with her husband Mark to the school. When they arrived, it seemed like a "burial ground". A stunned grief pervaded the school. The girls who had been rescued were leaving in a hurry with their parents. The property of the girls was scattered in the mud. Some parents of the girls who had been abducted were rolling on the ground wailing for their lost daughters. She searched desperately among the rescued girls for Charlotte but couldn't see her. She found Sister Rachele who couldn't bear to establish eye contact with her. This told her that Sister Rachele had no good news for her. Her heart sank as it dawned on her that Charlotte was one of the thirty still missing. Then she saw the list of the missing and found Charlotte's name on it. Words can't describe the horror she felt as it dawned on her that her beloved, beautiful, intelligent Charlotte was now in the merciless hands of these monsters. What would become of her?

The grief and fear in the following days was hard for Angelina to bear. Nightmare scenarios plagued her mind night and day. She felt that she should do more than pray. After discussions with Sister Rachele, she decided that she would form "The Concerned Parents Association" (CPA). Sister Rachele and the other parents joined in the advocacy work. Their aim was to work for the release of their own daughters and campaign for all the thousands of abducted children. Their two main weapons would be prayer and publicity. The appalling situation in Northern Uganda had gone largely unnoticed by the outside world. This was now about to change. Angelina is an intelligent, determined and articulate person. For her, the best way of coping with her grief and worry was to plunge herself into the work of the pressure group she had formed.

Their daughters became known around the world as the "Aboke Girls". In the course of the next few years, the news of the Aboke Girls became the most widely known horror story of the entire conflict. The CPA appealed to Pope John Paul II, who condemned the abductions, therefore drawing international attention to the incident and the situation in Northern Uganda in general. On March 7th 1997, President Museveni wrote to United Nations Secretary General, Kofi Annan, describing the plight of the Aboke Girls. In June 1997, Sister Rachele and members of the CPA met with LRA commanders in Juba, Sudan. After originally denying that they held the girls, they then said they would release them if the Ugandan military declared a ceasefire. The Ugandan government had no alternative but to reject the proposal and stated that they were not responsible for anything that may happen to the girls.

Sister Rachele and Angelina Atyam have, between the two of them, met the UN Special Representative for children and armed conflicts, Olara Otunnu, U.S. First Lady Hilary Clinton, the UN Secretary General Kofi Annan, the President of Uganda Yoweri Museveni, the Pope, members of the European Parliament, former South African President Nelson Mandela, Libyan President Muammar al-Gaddafi, Sudanese President Omar al-Bashir, and Zimbabwean President Robert Mugabe, as well as numerous diplomats of other nations to highlight the captivity of their girls. The Aboke Girls came to symbolise the wider horror of tens of thousands of children snatched from their villages, many of them never to return. The children suffered and died and their parents suffered pain and loss in absolute obscurity. Only God knows the full story and when the time comes, He will judge those responsible. It is sad to realise that if Westerners are not involved and their oil supply is not threatened, this sort of conflict receives little or no attention in the Western world's media or from their governments.

Underpinning all this effort was prayer. After the school resumed, the students and staff met every day at six in the evening and prayed for the release of the girls. The parents met in their churches and prayed frequently with nights of prayer, sometimes with long periods of fasting. Why didn't the God of the whole of the universe, in who was all power, release their daughters? They had no answer to this question, but nothing prevented them from continuing to pray and trust God. Born out of extreme suffering, their prayers and worship were now elevated to higher plains giving glory to God. They worshipped in spite of the tragic circumstances. They entered that realm in which Job found himself in the Old Testament, where all he could say in the midst of terrible suffering was,

> *"Though He slay me, yet will I trust Him"*
>
> (Job 13:15).

Occasionally, snippets of news about the girls would filter through to their parents. In Africa, this really is the "Bush telegraph". One day the news came to Angelina that her daughter Charlotte was pregnant. She eventually gave birth to a son. Angelina's deep anger turned to a rage and hatred inside her. How could this happen? Why did they still hold her daughter? She continued to pray with the other parents.

In one meeting God began to speak to them in a way they didn't expect. God said,

"Come unto me all you that are heavy laden and I will give you rest."

Angelina thought to herself, *We certainly need rest; our hearts are in turmoil and filled with anger.* As the Spirit of God began to speak into her heart she realised that she needed to be broken. Her resentment, her fight, her anger was eating her up. Angelina and the others had to be reconciled to men before they could experience peace from God. It was a deep and difficult lesson to have to learn.

Angelina realised that whenever she heard the Acholi language, it would make her angry. An Acholi visited her neighbour and she told her that if her daughter came back with an Acholi baby, she would throw it away. She hated all Acholi people because of Charlotte's abduction and suffering. It was that powerful traditional tribal hatred that was trying to take over her heart. She was full of resentment and bitterness.

God spoke to her in the night as she was praying and said, "Angelina, why are you praying with all this anger and bitterness? Your mind is clouded. You cannot receive anything from me this way."

Suddenly, she saw it all. Satan was trying to snare her into the very hatred that had blighted her country for centuries. She now began a period of deep repentance. She asked God to renew her heart and to give her that godly peace which passes all understanding. She now knew the key that would eventually resolve the situation. She had to be like God and forgive those who had sinned against her and her daughter. Later, a young visitor came to her house who spoke Acholi. As she heard the language, she realised that it no longer made her angry. In fact it was a pleasing sound, almost like music. Through this she now knew that she had forgiven those men who had her daughter.

She began to share this powerful message with the other parents. They too should forgive the very ones who had taken their daughters. She stood amongst the parents and prayed in a loud voice:

"Lord, I forgive Joseph Kony, I forgive the rebels, I forgive the ones who took my daughter. I forgive them with all my heart. Lord, I set them free in your Name – open a door whereby they may come out of the bush."

They then made a covenant with God: "Lord, we will wait on you. We will not consult another god – whether we see the girls again or not, we will wait on you, O God."

Mark Odongo, Angelina's husband, was deep in prayer one night and God gave him a vision – he saw beautiful flowers and as he admired them, God spoke into his heart, saying, "You see these beautiful flowers? They are not yours, they are mine and I will look after them."

God was speaking about the Aboke Girls.

Then it was time for patience and prayer. Now the powers of darkness could be broken by sustained prayer, not hindered by anger and bitterness. Their forgiveness carried power in the heavenly realms. The parents could be excused for thinking that after such a powerful spiritual victory, they would soon see their girls. Alas, it was not to be. Months, then years, went by, but still they clung to God's word. Although the advocacy work became known around the world, in many ways this turned out to be counter-productive. Angelina and Sister Rachele, with a government delegation, even met with Kony and asked him to release the girls. He refused, but offered to release Charlotte to Angelina if she would give up her international campaigning, which was putting him under pressure from the Sudan government. After a moment's thought, Angelina made an incredible decision. Although desperate to get her daughter back, she refused his offer. She insisted that all the girls should be released. Nothing less was acceptable. Her decision could cost her daughter's life, she knew that, but God had spoken to them and she couldn't bring herself to take the easy option. She was the group's leader and their champion; they were relying on her to finish the task she had so courageously begun.

They had now become political pawns. Because of the worldwide attention on these girls, Kony ordered that they must be under special guard at all times lest any of them escape. Escapes by the children were not uncommon. It was virtually impossible to guard thousands of children round the clock. The main thing that kept them captive was the fear of the brutality they would receive if they were caught attempting to escape. It was also realised that the Aboke Girls were more intelligent than most and were capable of working out ingenious schemes to escape.

Things began to turn as a result of a much greater spiritual victory. It was a victory that was yet to unfold. In fact, the spiritual victory of the CPA may have been the catalyst for greater things to come. Meanwhile, both the parents and the girls continued to suffer. It would be eight long years before Angelina would see Charlotte again. During this time, some escaped and some were killed. A number of them became mothers.

One day in 2004, after years of plotting how to escape, even trying to escape without it looking as though she was, Charlotte was marching through the bush with a large group of rebels. She was now a mother of two boys. She had one with her and had become temporarily separated from the other. As they were walking through very thick bush, the weary line had become long and broken in places. At a turn in the path, the column marched straight on, but she and her son – as if absentmindedly – took the left turn. The guards who had been assigned to watch her were inattentive. She kept walking, occasionally looking back. On they went until she realised they were not being followed. Then she began to run, carrying her son. The hard life in the bush now became an asset in terms of fitness and stamina as she forged ahead through the thick bush. Thorns and branches lashed at her body. The baby strapped to her back bounced up and down as she ran. The thought of what would happen to her if she was now caught, drove her on. She asked directions as she travelled and eventually found her way home. The Ugandan army soon located the other child and reunited him with his mother.

When mother and daughter first spotted each other in July after Charlotte's escape, they did what Angelina had dreamed about for so long. Later she closed her eyes as she recalled the moment. "She ran to me and I ran to her. She screamed and I screamed. For some time, we couldn't talk. We only cried. It was the best cry of my life."

Charlotte revealed that she had known nothing about her mother's dealings with the rebels or of her captors' offer to release her years before. She said she just guessed that her mother had to be working for her release. She was amazed that through it all, her mother had travelled the world meeting great leaders, trying to secure her freedom.

"I know she tried to get me out," said Charlotte, softly spoken and clearly pained. "... but it took so long."

As mother and daughter sat across from each other recounting their remarkable tale, it was clear that there was tension in the air.

"I know she's angry at me," Angelina said, looking across the room at her daughter, now a grown woman and mother of two.

"She has a right to be angry. She had wanted to change schools. She felt unsafe. I didn't listen."

Charlotte would not acknowledge as much. "I don't have much anger," she said.

"I know she didn't want it to happen. She just wanted a good future for me. But then this happened."

Exactly what happened over the last eight years, Charlotte largely glossed over. The rebels forced her to stone another captive to death. She tells of a beating so severe she almost died when she had two hundred lashes and lost consciousness. But it is a period that she clearly wishes to forget. It is all far too painful to talk about. It was in discussing the future that Charlotte's face filled with emotion. She had been a top student in a top school, with so many dreams. Now she has two unplanned children and no way of independently supporting them. As with all Africans, the past is gone and so has its importance. It is time to think of the now and contemplate the future.

She still longs to study again, although her previous decision to become a doctor is now lost.

"I've seen too much blood to work in a hospital" she says.

Returning to St. Mary's as a student was also out of the question. Charlotte visited her old campus for the next anniversary of the raid, but she said she could never spend another night in that dorm.

Angelina has become a doting grandmother, winning the love of her daughter's two young sons. She also cares for Charlotte trying to give her some of the love she was so long denied. Angelina had changed too over the eight years that her daughter was gone. She was now an activist as well as a mother. She has met world leaders, spoken at the United Nations in New York and in foreign capitals about this awful and much-ignored war. Her fight for the return of other Aboke Girls as well as the many other abducted children was far from over.

"I've got Charlotte back, but what about all the other parents?" Angelina asked.

"They are suffering like I suffered. When I got my daughter it was good, so very good, but it was like getting a few drops from the ocean. It didn't completely quench my thirst."

Upon emerging from captivity, Charlotte underwent an army debriefing and then counselling at the Sister Rachele Rehabilitation Centre, which was set up in honour of the Italian nun who in risking her own life, saved so many of her girls. Such courage deserves recognition.

Others had escaped as pressure on the LRA made it more difficult for them to keep everyone in order. Many of their own mid-level commanders deserted. Six St Mary's girls are believed to remain in captivity, some are dead. Every year the school holds a sombre ceremony on the anniversary of the raid. Students say prayers and walk silently, clutching candles, from the dorms to the memorial site. The subsequent students learned the names of the missing girls, after repeating them so often in their prayers. They had never met Caroline or Jacqueline or Susan or Miriam or Catherine or Sylvia, but they said they felt that they knew them and hoped to meet them one day.

One remarkable postscript to this record is the story of one of the girls from St Mary's named Janet. She escaped in 2005. She had been given to one of the lower commanders as his "wife". He was only a couple of years older than she was. He too had been snatched from his village and family. As they lived together in the LRA camp they fell in love with each other. A year later, he too managed to escape and join Janet. They soon had a formal marriage ceremony to make everything legal. When her father was asked how he felt about his son-in-law, he said, "He's not my son-in-law. He's my *son.*"

Such is the power of forgiveness.

CHAPTER 10

The Ministry Begins

For Beatrice and John, the months that followed at Kaniki Bible College were wonderful. Kaniki is a beautiful place, adorned with tropical flowers and shrubs, some indigenous but many brought in from other parts of Africa. Peter and Clara Marie Pedersen, and Jorn and Elizabeth Pedersen – Peter's brother and his wife – were the core of the college staff. Jorn had originally been sent to Zambia by the Danish government as a teacher. At the school where he first worked, he preached the Gospel to the children and many came to Christ. It is not an exaggeration to say that they experienced revival in that school.

The two brothers shared a vision for a Bible College in the Copperbelt area of Zambia and built up Kaniki College from nothing. The site had been just wild bush. Their denomination, the Danish Apostolic Church, funded the construction of a campus that was in itself a testimony to God. They believed that excellence was something that glorified God. The ten acre site has buildings of a good standard, an abundance of tropical flowers and trees and even a swimming pool.

It is the ethos of Kaniki that makes it so special. The students undertake a two year Bible-based course, but each student is also discipled in their own Christian life. The emphasis is on building character and integrity. This is the great need in the African churches. Kaniki turns out men and women of God who live godly, honest and transparent lives that glorify Him.

John and Beatrice made lots of good friends and impressed all who came to know them. The two boys, Donald and Prince, lived in a happy and secure environment. John's powerful leadership gifting was recognised by the college staff and as the time came for them to graduate, people wondered what kind of ministry God would use them in when they returned to Uganda.

John graduated with the full diploma and Beatrice a certificate because she had missed the first term. The plan was for her to return at some point to complete the other term. The journey back home was very different from the stressful experience Beatrice had had on the long journey to come to Kaniki. They had enough money and knew what things would cost. It was the same combination of buses and trains and endless hours of travelling, but more relaxed now that they were a family together. They booked a second class compartment with sleeping bunks on the long train journey and took turns to sleep. At Dar es Salaam, they stayed two nights in a small hotel to rest the children and relax and did the same in Nairobi. John had been appalled to hear Beatrice's story of her journey down and he was determined that the journey back would be more like a holiday. John's commanding presence took away any fear. They were excited to be going home and seeing their family and friends. They now had two little boys who would certainly be the centre of great interest as they did the rounds to greet everyone.

While they had been at Kaniki, John had corresponded with Donald Hemingway in New Zealand and told him that he had a vision to begin a Bible College in Soroti. Donald replied saying that he had the same vision and would do his best to raise funds and help. Donald sent money to a friend, ahead of John and Beatrice's return, with instructions to find a house to rent and pay the normal deposit of six months rent. This would give the family a place to return to. Unfortunately, the money was "borrowed" for something else and when they arrived, there was no house. After four cramped days with Beatrice's father, they had to move to John's family home in Otuboi village thirty miles north of Soroti, while they planned their next move.

Their arrival was a big event for the family. Everyone had to be visited or came to pay a visit. Beatrice's family too; everyone had to see the children and be brought up to date on everything that had happened. They prayed for guidance. John had so many things that he wanted to do and it was difficult to know which one to begin with. Kaniki had opened his eyes to a wide range of ministries a pastor could be involved in. There were many needs in the community. Education was one of the most important. To anyone observing John over the next few years, it would seem that his answer to the question of which of all the ideas in his mind to pursue, was to attempt all of them at the same time! John was a man in a hurry.

After two or three weeks in the village they realised that this was not what they had been called by God to do. They had to get back to town. Again they crowded back into Simon Peter's home in town. Donald Hemingway was still visiting the area and they had discussions with him. He had very little money with which to help. Eventually he agreed that he could rent a smaller, cheaper house. This would serve both as accommodation for the family, accommodation for the students and as the college! This was really starting small, but it was a start. They recruited seven male students for a one-year course. These first students paid a small fee of about £10 a term. This amount is a struggle for poor Africans to find without a job. Some of them were not able to keep paying the fees and during the second and third terms paid reduced amounts. This is a very African story. Trying to do good things with hardly any funds is a common feature of life in this continent. Beatrice cooked for everyone and looked after the children. They were like an extended family. John did most of the teaching and Beatrice too helped with teaching. The next year they recruited ten students, again all living in their house.

Back in New Zealand, Donald raised more money for the college. A second house was rented for the family, leaving the first one as the students' accommodation. While this was progressing John planted their first church, meeting in the garage of the house. When the church became too large for the garage, they rented a room in a local school and the garage then became the lecture room for the college. Its name was "Vision Bible College". The year was 1995.

John and Beatrice saw that there was a great need in the district to train young women. When girls left school, most could not find a job. Many of them either married young or became pregnant. They needed a skill to offer to an employer. The solution was to begin a training school for girls, offering secretarial training and tailoring. They rented premises in town at a place called "Corner House". John had a way of gathering people to his cause. His leadership drew people. Increasing numbers were getting involved. As soon as the girl's training college began, John wanted to build two secondary schools. The first one was in Otuboi, which was his home village. The second was in Soroti and called Hillside. It began, but didn't last very long. It was under-funded, the buildings were of a temporary type and it seemed that many others were opening schools in Soroti. These were not just for educational provision, they were also a business. Many schools in Africa are operating on this basis. He raised money wherever he could. They bought a plot of land for agricultural use where the Bible students worked to grow some of their own food.

Places at the girl's business college were in demand. However, the premises were inadequate and they obviously needed to pay rent. Simon Peter had a large, partly constructed house on his own property, which had been there when he purchased it. If it could be completed, it would make a good location for the business school because of its size. He didn't have the money to complete the building himself, he would need help. The project had good prospects because there was obviously a demand for the training and students were prepared to pay the fees to gain the valuable training. Virtually all the graduates were finding jobs in businesses all over the Teso region. Beatrice tells how, even to this day, as she travels around Teso, young women will come running to her and say, "Mommy, do you remember me? I trained at the college and now I am working in such and such a department or business."

One thing was certain, John and Beatrice Omese were the centre of a whirlwind of activity in Soroti. Somehow, Beatrice managed to fit in giving birth to a third son, Joshua.

John had founded an Elim Foursquare Gospel Alliance church before going to Zambia. When he came back, junior pastors looked after that church. Students from Vision Bible School were trained by John and sent out to villages to plant churches for one week of evangelism. In Africa you can plant a new church in a village just by going there to preach and talk to people. If a pastor preaches under the same tree each Sunday, most of the village will turn up and they have a church. They would then gradually put up a building. About thirty-two churches were planted in this way where John cared for and supervised the pastors.

It was at this stage that Peter Pedersen requested the help of John Barry, the CEO of a UK-based mission called *REAP International Ministries*. REAP stood for "Riverside European and African projects". The mission was sponsored by Riverside Church in Birmingham. The original idea for a church-based missions programme had come from the Pastor, Nick Cuthbert. Nick and his wife Lois gave their encouragement and helped find the funds for REAP. The ministry had grown far wider than the church members and facilitated over seven hundred people going on teams to Africa over a twelve year period. Kaniki Bible College was one of the partners of REAP in Zambia. During one of his research trips to Kaniki, Peter Pedersen invited John Barry round to his bungalow for coffee and began to tell him all about John and Beatrice and their fast developing ministry in Soroti. Peter knew that REAP regularly sent short-term teams to Mozambique, Malawi, Zimbabwe and Zambia. He asked John if he would send a team to Soroti. He replied that he would try his best to do so.

John Barry called in the help of his good friends and co-workers, Paul and Tessa Settatree. They lived in West Wales and had been assisting REAP by undertaking research trips to Africa. REAP had a policy that they would never send a team – which were mostly university students – to any location without good research beforehand. In the early years of the REAP ministry, John Barry and his wife had undertaken the research trips themselves. As the work expanded, there were just too many locations for them to visit and still keep up the administration work in the office. They needed the help of people whose opinion they trusted. Paul and Tessa fitted the profile for a good research team. They had sound judgement, knowledge of Africa, vision and passion. They readily agreed to visit Soroti and spy out the land. Paul was particularly keen because he had worked in Uganda as a young man on "Voluntary Service Overseas" and he had retained an interest and affection for the "Pearl of Africa". They would return with the answers REAP needed before they could send teams. Questions such as: Did the local partners seem reliable? Where would the team be accommodated? Where would they eat, wash, relax in the evenings? What about transport, building materials, medical assistance, security, laundry, clean water etc? When all the assurances that REAP needed were given, they could recruit a team.

Paul and Tessa had asked John and Beatrice about a team coming to help them and what work they would most like them to do and the answer was to complete the business training college. Short term missions were very popular at this time among the Christian Unions in British universities and finding a team of seven for the summer of 1998 was not difficult. Jon Curtis, experienced in mission work, was the team leader recruited for this team going to Soroti.

A few months later John Barry made his first visit to Soroti with the Chairman of the REAP board, Steve Botham. By the time Steve and John arrived they were able to view the business college, the partly erected Hillside school, the school at Otuboi, cashew nut processing, training of the newly acquired oxen and Vision Bible College. Steve caused much laughter by accepting the challenge to man the plough as the two new oxen were encouraged to attempt ploughing for the first time. Steve was dragged all over the place as the oxen alternated obeying the rods urging them forward or attempted to escape sideways. The group of local people watching could hardly stand up for laughing. Watching a *muzungu* (white person) make a fool of himself is one of the best entertainments in Africa. Steve proved himself to be a good sport, as well as being a competent and enthusiastic chairman of the mission board.

Of all the places they visited on that trip, the one that stood out most in their minds was the school at Otuboi. It had been named "Trinity College". The original idea came from the villagers for a "Parents' School". This is a school initiated by the parents. Otuboi is a large village with over five thousand people and encompasses many others from the surrounding rural area. They had no school in or even near Otuboi. While preparation for this team was underway, John Barry applied to the American Embassy in Kampala for a grant to build the school in Otuboi. They donated $12,000 which was enough for the basic building to be erected.

Their visit to the school was scheduled to be on a Saturday, which was not a normal school day. Nevertheless, the children had been asked to come to school this day in their uniforms, just to greet their visitors from England. They were not able to arrive at the school until four in the afternoon and the children had been waiting for them for most of the day. About eighty pupils assembled in two lines and sang several songs for their special visitors. Looking at the children they realised that almost everyone from John's village was very tall. Even the teenage girls were approaching six feet in height. Some of the boys played homemade instruments and one of the youngest girls sang a solo. Her song was one specially written to greet them. It was very moving. After this, Steve and John both had to make encouraging speeches; as they did everywhere they went. It is a Ugandan custom. It was a wonderful experience for both of them to be there.

John and Steve had been given a ride in a pastor's pickup. As they prepared to board the vehicle to return to Soroti they were asked to give a lift to some of the children who lived in villages along the main road to Soroti. The pastor agreed and an impossible number of pupils piled into the open back of the vehicle. They pulled slowly away with the flattened springs creaking and the vehicle barely under control. Once again the Toyota pickup truck proved itself to be the world's toughest vehicle.

The arrangement was that when someone wanted to get off, they would bang the roof of the cab. John wondered how far the children walked each day to come to school, so he noted the mileage on the dashboard. They stopped at many villages along the road and one or two children jumped off each time. As the miles ticked by, John was becoming more alarmed at the distance. He prayed a really silly prayer,

"Lord, please don't let it be any further for these children."

When the last two children jumped off the truck, he noted that they were twelve miles from the school! John asked the pastor if these children walked that far every day. He assured him that they did. They left home in the dark at four in the morning and walked four hours to arrive at school by eight. They left school at four in the afternoon and arrived home after dark at eight. The pastor saw John's amazed expression and said, "That's right. Sixteen hours away from home and no food!"

Such is the hunger for education in Africa! Soon, very basic dormitories for the girls and boys were set up to save the long distance walk each day that some of the children faced.

CHAPTER 11

Evil at the Door

During 2003 many rumours and horror stories of LRA activity came to Otuboi village. In the back of everyone's mind was the mental preparation for what they should do if the violence threatened their village. They would grab everything that they could carry and run. The rumours became a reality when villagers saw refugees passing through Otuboi as they fled south. Faces taut with fear, their body language determined, they warned everyone to flee. They told how the LRA were killing any men that they found and many of the women. Some of the women were being taken as slaves to carry loads. All the children aged between seven and eighteen years old were also being taken. A bow wave of fear spread before the advancing rebels. Kony, having in his own mind conquered the far north, was now making a bid for Teso and in particular, Soroti town. He had proved to himself and his strange army that he was immune from the attempts of the Ugandan People's Liberation Army (UPLA) to stop him. Confident in the power he possessed – or rather, possessed him – his collection of several thousand heavily armed thugs and children marched south. They knew that many fled before them telling the stories of the atrocities they had committed en route. Thus, fear became a weapon to intimidate and terrify all who lay before them.

Some of the refugees had relatives on whom they would descend, confident that ancient ties of clan and family would bring forth what little help could be mustered. Most had nowhere to go and didn't know what would become of them; only saving their lives mattered at this time. They carried a few belongings, and some had even been forced to flee without a child, a wife, or aged parents, not knowing the fate of their family members. For most, the end of their journey would be squalid refugee camps for IDPs. About 400,000 people in total were displaced from Teso alone. In total from other areas more than a million were displaced.

The insurgents had heard about the new Trinity College and the dormitories. This would be a great prize for them. Fortunately, the rebels could not advance in secrecy. Those that had managed to escape southward in time forewarned the school of their advance. As the rebels approached Otuboi, they grabbed a couple of people who had been too slow or too infirm to run and found out where the dormitories were located. They were disappointed. With only a few hours to spare, the children, led by their courageous teachers had fled to hide in the bush. The next day they marched south to the next village of Kalaki, on the main road towards Soroti. The Otuboi school building was now abandoned to the LRA.

The LRA groups halted in Otuboi. To go further south would need reinforcements because they would need to overcome the town of Soroti with its 60,000 population. From Otuboi they raided right up to the outer suburbs of the town, from where they were driven back. As Soroti filled up with IDPs and the children from Trinity College reached Kalaki, fear began to turn to anger. In one of Uganda's previous internal struggles for power, a militia group called "The Arrow Boys" had fought against a previous government. The "Arrow" in the name symbolised fighters who kept a straight path in the direction of their goal. They had been disbanded, but the veterans still lived in this area – and, just as importantly, still knew how to use a gun. Previously they had been part of a movement called "FOBA" which stood for "Force Obote Back". After Milton Obote had been overthrown, a movement was launched in his own tribal area to bring him back. Obote was an evil man, not much better than Idi Amin. However, in Africa the tribal system is all powerful: "*My leader, right or wrong.*" This rule also applies to someone's tribe, clan, family and brother.

If the Arrow Boys could be reassembled into a fighting force, maybe the LRA could be stopped. They needed leadership, a motive and guns. Several local leaders stepped up to organise a resistance. Most prominent among these was Mr. Musa Ecweru, who was the Resident District Commissioner for Kasesa District. He had previously been a leader in the now defunct Ugandan People's Army. The motivation came as the insurgency was perceived as a tribal conflict, thus igniting powerful and ancient instincts in the people. *"This LRA is an Acholi problem. How dare they come and attack us Iteso. We will fight back."*

Mr. Musa went to President Museveni and asked for arms. He told the President that he couldn't continue his work and watch his people being killed and their children abducted. He was Iteso himself, he even originated from the same village as Beatrice. The President was persuaded, even though it is a dangerous thing to arm any militia in Africa. He could see that Mr. Musa was an outstanding leader and appointed him as District Commissioner of Soroti district with permission to resurrect the Arrow Boys and arm them. This would also help the Ugandan Defence Force who were so frequently frustrated in trying to fight the LRA because they simply couldn't find the raiding parties that attacked villages. They would melt back into the bush in classic guerrilla tactics. Some way had to be found to overcome the elusiveness of the LRA.

Mr. Musa spoke on the radio to appeal for recruits who knew how to use a gun. The word quickly spread and recruits began to enlist. Recruitment began in the middle of 2003 and he soon had a force of 2,000. The militia peaked in January 2004 with 12,000. Their ranks also contained young teenagers and even some women. They were given some very basic training and a gun to fight with. Every village in Teso raised a troop of "Arrow Boys". Mr. Musa led from the front. He and his two brothers led many patrols north to confront the LRA. They had a few armoured troop carriers at their disposal. They were often ambushed by rebels but always fought them off. As the ambushers were scattered, numerous children were released from their camps.

Now the LRA had a problem. The enemy they now faced were everywhere. They also knew their own area well, whereas the LRA didn't.

As with conflicts the world over, people who are defending their homes and families fight with much greater courage and motivation. Some had already lost their children or other relatives and were angry and determined. Kony's rag-tag army of drugged-up thugs were no match for the Arrow Boys. Eventually they were driven out of Teso.

Mr. Musa visited many churches and asked all the congregations to pray. He told them that he would battle with guns, but they must battle in prayer. Many special prayer meetings were convened. People fasted and prayed during their lunchtimes. Mr. Musa gained a lot of respect when he closed down all the video stores in Soroti that were stocking pornography – which was all of them!

One of the ways the LRA commanders used witchcraft was to call down very heavy rain on otherwise fine days, as they approached a village. This would drive the people into their huts. Consequently, when the LRA unit attacked, the people were trapped inside. Normally they would have been outside or in their fields and would have seen the LRA coming, enabling most to flee into the bush. Once the prayer campaign began, this power was broken. The rebels lost every battle with the Arrow Boys. Kony lost about seventeen of his commanders in these skirmishes.

At the height of the LRA insurgency into Teso in 2003, they approached Soroti and prepared to attack it. The population feared that the town would be overrun and many lives lost. At this time Beatrice had a dream through which God spoke to her. In the dream she had been captured by the LRA while she was walking with her youngest son, John Paul, on her back. One of the LRA women was put in charge of guarding her. She spoke to this lady and said, "Let us both escape."

They ran away and came across an old house, strongly built with a large padlock on the door. They knocked on the door and asked to be let in. The owner said that the rebels were coming and that they were going to lock the house and go to Soroti. Beatrice said that they had been walking a long way and were too tired to go further. The occupants let them in and they went up to the top of the house to pray. As they prayed, the power of God came down and in an instant she found herself in church surrounded by people worshipping God. Then she heard a voice saying,

"Have you seen the power of God? This will be the solution to this war."

Beatrice shared this prophetic dream with many churches and widows groups. Jesus was their refuge. People realised that the solution was going to be in prayer. One of the widows came to Beatrice and suggested that the groups of widows should all flee south to Kampala. Beatrice told her that if they stayed and fought the battle in prayer, everything would be all right.

"We will run to Jesus."

Rumours began to spread in Soroti that the LRA were about to attack the town. Many simply refused to believe it. Some treated it as a joke. They just couldn't believe that the LRA would dare to try such a bold strategy. After all, the army was in town and so were the Arrow Boys. As a precaution, many who lived on the outskirts of town came into the centre at night and slept on the streets. Some visited the bars to drink Ajono, the favourite local brew of Teso.

On the night of September 30th 2003, at approximately 1am, the LRA came in force in an attempt to take the town. The government troops were mostly stationed at the small airport known as "The Flying School". This has an unusually long runway at over 6,000 feet. The Flying School was originally built by the British Overseas Aircraft Corporation to train its pilots in tropical flying techniques. The LRA knew they must capture this strategic place if they were to succeed. The town was defended by both the UPDF troops and the Arrow Boys. Every person in town woke as the bullets flew through the normally quiet street and the night sky was lit up like a fireworks display. Every attack by these hardened, drug-fuelled rebels was driven off in battles and skirmishes that lasted throughout the night.

The next day, many tried to flee the town fearing that the attacks would continue. Buses and Matatus filled to capacity. Unscrupulous drivers hiked the fares. Over the next week, skirmishes could be heard as small local attacks around the outskirts of the town took place each night at 1am. The bars did a roaring trade as alcohol became the people's sleeping pill. But the initiative now was with the defenders who grew in confidence. During the day, people went about their normal business as if nothing was happening. More than two hundred died. Noted for their bravery were the Arrow Boys who had fought like lions. Their courage is now remembered each year in Soroti on "Arrow Day".

Having beaten off this full-force attack, the UPLA and the Arrow group were now able to take the battle to the enemy and gradually the LRA were driven out of Teso. It became clear to the churches that the military victory was made possible by the spiritual victory – in prayer.

The LRA were not defeated; they still terrorised the areas further north. However, they had been expelled from Teso. For them to finally be defeated it was going to need an amazing spiritual intervention from the churches to put an end to what was essentially a spiritually-empowered force. The combination of prayer and military resistance had won the day in Teso. It was an indication as to how the final battle, on a much broader canvas, would finally be won.

The people of Soroti town did their best to continue life as normal while hearing of the violence further north. Refugees were pouring into town and the local churches, the local authority and aid agencies did their best to resettle them in IDP camps around the edge of town.

Most of John Omese's projects continued to be developed. John had been keen that other young pastors should attend Kaniki Bible College for the same standard of training that he and Beatrice had benefited from. The next person to study at Kaniki was Francis Alemu. He was also Iteso and just as tall as John. However, there the similarity ended. Francis was in many ways an opposite of John. He is a gentle giant, quiet, slow to speak and thoughtful. He had been trained as a bookkeeper which suited his meticulous approach to tasks. John knew that to develop all the projects that buzzed around in his mind, he would need the help of Francis to run the Bible College. He was followed by Patrick Orotin, yet another Iteso giant with a ready smile and cheerful disposition. All studied at Kaniki and returned with a determination to establish the same quality of teaching and good character in a Bible college in Soroti.

After the insurgency was driven from Teso and John Omese had died, the parents of Otuboi elected Beatrice to continue to manage Trinity College. It took a while to get it running again, but eventually the teachers and the pupils returned. It was a great victory. Initially there was no money to pay the teachers, so they taught as volunteers to enable the school to recommence.

CHAPTER 12

The Promise of God

John's Omese's funeral took place three days after his sudden death. He was taken to Faith Mission church so that the people in the town, as well as friends and relatives could view his body in the traditional African way. He was one of the most well known people in Soroti. Then he was taken home to Otuboi, his ancestral village, to be buried in his family plot. More than a thousand mourners, some from other districts, came to see the body and mourn his passing.

After the funeral, Simon Peter and Bishop John Etiu – a cousin of John Omese – held a meeting to decide how the ministry and projects should continue. Eventually it was decided that a trust should be formed. The various projects that John had begun were mostly still in a development stage. The most advanced was the business school. Pastor Santos John Labeja owned a local school called Central Academy. It had been founded by John Omese and Santos before John went to Kaniki, and so Santos was asked to join the trust. His school was only half completed. It was designed to accommodate a large number of children and they had enough buildings partially completed. They had four walls and a roof, but that was all. Some classrooms needed a floor and every wall needed plastering inside and out. This was without any equipment or furniture. The classes that were taught there were operating in poor conditions. This for most Africans is better than no school at all. Then there were about thirty churches in the district that John had planted. John had appointed Pastors to each one, with John acting as their leader and teacher.

Matthew Steel, from the UK, had also completed the course at Kaniki Bible College. The college occasionally has one or two European students. After graduating he felt called to go to Soroti to work as a missionary, working with John and Beatrice. Peter Pedersen had shared with him the need for help in managing the various projects. He stayed two years and did a wonderful job helping organise the administration. He developed the agricultural side of things and began marketing cashew nuts and growing peppers, which were in demand in the West because of the rapid expansion of the "Chicken Tikka" phenomenon and related exotic dishes. Peter Pedersen, the former Principal of Kaniki, has always followed up on his graduates to see how they are getting on and to help and encourage them in any way. He and Clara Marie visited Soroti twice while John was still alive and continue to visit ever since.

As with most widows in Africa, Beatrice now found herself without much income. She couldn't work because she had four young sons to care for. John Paul, the youngest, was still a small baby. Some of the REAP team members who had worked with John and Beatrice on a short term team, having heard about John's death, and knowing the financial situation Beatrice was in, decided to help out on a long-term basis. Her biggest burden was the monthly rent for their house. School fees for the children were also very difficult and would increase as the boys grew older and advanced in their education. Beatrice's landlady, Margaret Esilu, was sympathetic to her plight but her husband and his two other wives had all died, and in their culture she was now responsible for more than ten children. The rent from the house was her only income.

There are many destitute widows in Africa and we can't help them all. However, when you have come to know and love one, you just can't walk away saying, "May God bless you." Even with some help from her friends in the UK, Beatrice was falling behind with the rent and she realised that she must move out of the house. So with great sadness she asked her father if she could go back to the family home. She and her four boys were given one small room to share in a house that was already crowded with other relatives sharing. It is a tradition in Africa, that if a relative comes and asks for help – either financial or for accommodation – the powerful family code demands that you help if you possibly can. Anyone with a home is bound to help a relative who is homeless. For Beatrice there was another cultural aspect. She felt ashamed to have to go home to her parents as an adult and a mother. Once you have left your family home, you are expected to make your own way in the world.

She had been an outstanding pupil at school and student at college. She had made a good marriage to a prominent member of the community, she had travelled to another country to study at an excellent Bible College, she had friends overseas and her future had looked wonderful. Now she was alone and her only income was from friends in the UK. She had also now lost her family home and she felt ashamed of what her life had become.

To add to the difficulty of their confined living space, a neighbour's son was exerting a bad influence over her boys. He was a little older than her oldest and he was very naughty. In fact "naughty" is a mild word to use about him; he was behaving very badly and he knew it. On one occasion he gave her boys condoms to play with, to blow up as balloons. Beatrice was horrified. She didn't even know if they had been used or not. So many people had AIDS in Uganda and it worried her. The boy even taunted Beatrice and told her that he was going to make her boys as bad has he was. It added to the frustration and humiliation she was experiencing. Her life was at an all time low.

She hated living in these conditions and desperately wanted her own house, to be able to live in peace with her boys and do the work of the Lord. In desperation she took the two oldest boys – who were the ones being most influenced by this bad boy – to a better school called Mjoyoyo School. It was residential and near the town of Jinja. This is about three hours journey by bus from Soroti. It was Beatrice's cousin, Moses, who recommended the school. His boys were happy there and had been talking to her boys about the school, so they were also keen to go. Importantly, they would be away from the bad influence, at least during the school term time. It took all the money she had to pay a term's fees in advance. Next time the fees were due, she could only pay half the fee for them. The school fees in Uganda are very small by our Western standards, but represent huge amounts to most Ugandans. She began to think that she might have made a mistake in putting the boys in the school and would have to bring them back to their previous local school in Soroti.

She wondered if she had, in fact, done this without God's blessing and just followed her own ideas. She knelt in prayer to ask God about it. The Lord brought to her mind a scripture,

"Do not be afraid, God is your helper."

She was greatly encouraged by this and went to the Head teacher of the school and promised to find the other half of the fees. Then God answered her prayers. One day Matthew came round and told her that Roddy Simson's mother had sent her some money. Roddy had led one of the REAP teams to Soroti. It was 400,000 Shillings. She was able to pay the remainder of the fees and also pay the next term in advance. God was being faithful to His promise. The next provision came on the heels of that one. Paul and Tessa's younger daughter Lucy was married to Oliver. They had had a wonderful wedding in their local church with a large marquee on Paul and Tessa's lawn for the reception. When Lucy gave birth to her first baby, Rosie, they sent money for two years school fees. Then when she gave birth to her second child, Edie, they again sent money enough for another two years. God was fulfilling His promise. Just as important, He was also doing a work of faith building in Beatrice herself. She was not alone. God was with her and would answer her prayers.

The children would sometimes ask her where their daddy was. There were photos of him in the house and this would remind them. He used to love playing with them. She told them that he had gone to heaven to be with God. They didn't really understand what this meant but accepted what they were told.

The problem of the bad neighbour inevitably reappeared when term finished and the boys had to come home for the holidays. This, combined with the unsuitable one-room accommodation, highlighted the main problem: she still needed a home of her own. When she met friends and relatives they would usually ask the inevitable questions: "Where are you now? Are you still living in the same house?"

Once again she felt ashamed of the answer that she had to give. She felt that she was letting her children down. God had miraculously provided the school fees; surely He could provide a place for them to stay. God had shown that He was with her and would answer her prayers. Now she began to pray earnestly for a much bigger miracle – her own house. Not one that required a lot of rent, but her own house.

Beatrice attended an overnight prayer meeting at AOG Church in Soroti. It was a joint fellowship meeting for all the Christians in town and was usually well attended. That night Beatrice found it difficult to pray. She felt restless and her mind rehearsed the problems of life that she and her four sons now faced. She took a walk outside the church in the cool night air to try to clear her mind. As she walked, she heard God speaking to her. The word came clearly and powerful. God told her that He was going to build her a house. Her heart leapt for joy at that word. Her own house, without the problem of rent. How could this be? Yet she was sure God had spoken. It would be a dream come true.

As she returned to the church she heard a different, mocking, voice: "Have you ever heard of a widow building a house? Have you ever seen a widow build a house? Have you ever heard of a widow, on her own, building a house?" Suddenly doubts filled her heart and she began to cry. Was it all a fantasy? Had she just imagined that God had spoken to her? She went outside again with a heavy heart. Then as she walked, God spoke to her again. He told her she needed to believe. God reminded her of Abraham and how he had to believe God for the impossible; that his descendants would be like the grains of sand on the shore. She knew she had to believe God and not listen to the doubts.

Beatrice held on tight to the word of God. This was her only hope; only God could meet her need. She expected things to start happening immediately, but they didn't. As often when God speaks a word, there follows a time of testing and learning patience, during which we have to continue to believe. Shortly after this, Beatrice attended an international prayer conference in Kampala. The two weeks of prayer included three days of prayer and fasting in the nearby mountains. Beatrice and a group of her widows went to the mountain. Everyone else had tents to sleep in, but as they had no tent, they slept in the open. During the night, light rain began to fall and they retreated under a tree and tried to sleep, feeling cold and wet. The next day they managed to find a tent the eight of them could sleep in for the remaining two nights.

In the last night of the fasting, Beatrice once again went out into the night to pray alone. She really needed a confirming word from God that His promise to her would be fulfilled. She particularly wanted to hear from God about a house to live in and fees for her boys to attend a suitable school. Again God spoke to her,

> *"Don't worry, I will build you a house; I will provide for your boys."*

Doubts still assailed her mind. She was in the midst of a fearsome spiritual battle to believe the word of God and she began to cry. Then, as if to confirm to her that she was in a battle and hearing from God, a strange thing happened to her. A "power" lifted her and threw her a distance of about five metres before she landed on the ground. She lay there without the strength to rise. She tried to get up but she fell. Once again she heard again the word from God:

> *"From this day I want you to believe that I will build you a house and take care of your boys."*

This strange experience became a sign to help her to believe in God's word. From this point on there were no more doubts, God was going to work on her behalf. As she lay on the ground in the deep darkness of the African night she began to repent of her unbelief. As she repented, her strength returned and she was able to get up after about forty minutes. The next morning they journeyed home. Back in Soroti she began to tell everyone that God was going to build her a house – she was sure of it.

Throughout this time, Beatrice was careful not to trust in man, but to trust in God. She deliberately didn't tell any of her friends in the UK. She didn't even tell them about her difficult living conditions in a single room. A month later, she had an enigmatic email from Paul Settatree, saying that he was coming to Uganda to do some work on her house. She wondered what house Paul was referring to. She had nothing for him to work on, not even a plot of land. She took the letter to her father to see what he thought of it. He told her just to wait and see what transpired.

Before Paul arrived in Uganda, God made His first move. A delegation of officials from the AOG church in the UK arrived in Soroti and told her that they had heard about John's death. John had been an AOG pastor and they wanted to help his widow. At the AOG conference in Nairobi they had given John $1,000 to help him in his ministry. John had given this to Beatrice for safe keeping. They asked if she still had this money. To their great surprise, she confirmed that she still had it. She was still keeping it safe for use in the ministry. They asked her what she needed. She told them about her need for a house, but she didn't even have a plot. They took the $1,000 with them back to the UK. Later, after consulting with others in the AOG in the UK, they added to this amount and made a bank transfer of enough money to buy a plot. Within days, a plot was purchased, plans drawn up and planning permission obtained. The British AOG paid for everything.

Just as hope was rising in her heart, Beatrice had a setback. The town officials told her that they were planning to build offices on her plot so she couldn't now have it, even though she had paid for it. She went to their offices to protest. When she saw that she was not going to get anywhere, she was about to begin crying. At the same moment she heard God speaking in her heart again:

"How dare you cry before these unbelievers? Don't cry, just trust in Me."

She held back her tears and went to the Land Board and explained what had happened. They told her not to worry. They would give her a substitute plot. This was unusual because the Land Board were selling the plots and her loss of a plot was officially not their fault or concern. She was given a new plot, but she had already spent money on the first one. She had purchased and placed hardcore stone on it. This now had to be transferred or she would lose it.

Shortly after this, Paul and Tessa Settatree arrived with a team of mostly young people from their church in Haverfordwest in West Wales, during the Easter holidays of 2002. Together with Moses, Beatrice's brother, they commenced work on the house. Like most African houses, it was a simple structure, one level and a single brick width of wall. By the time the team were ready to leave the walls were up to "ring beam" level – a course of reinforced concrete that tops off the walls which would otherwise be too weak to hold the roof and which has to withstand the storms of the wet season.

Paul's parting words to Beatrice were to continue to trust God. She knew that the job was less than half done, but a good start had been made. God was fulfilling His word to her. After Paul and Tessa returned home the progress on the house stopped for about two years. Then one day in West Wales, God spoke very clearly to Paul and Tessa that they needed to find the money to build Beatrice's house. It was urgent. The next day, they received news that a grandfather had left them some money. That was God's provision for completing the house. Sometimes in the Christian life, in obeying God's word, we often don't realise just how much we are instruments in His hands to fulfil His promises to others. Paul and Tessa and their team were vital instruments in Gods hands at this time; far more than they realised. Their compassion and determination were only a segment of a far larger purpose that God had in mind.

The fund-raising continued and the work progressed until the day came when Beatrice and her four children could move into their own, rent-free house. She was overjoyed. Her heart was full of gratitude to God, to Paul and Tessa and their friends in the UK. God's faithfulness and the provision of the house had a very profound effect in Beatrice's inner life as well as her outward circumstances. It had consequences that were to reverberate far beyond herself and her family. It raised Beatrice's level of faith in God. It was faith that was going to be exercised to believe God for much greater things in the future of her ministry. She looks back to this time and testifies that it all began there with God's provision of her house. If God could do this, if He was this faithful to her, nothing was impossible. Thousands of widows all around her were destitute with nowhere to live. Now, in her rapidly expanding ministry to these women, she could honestly say,

"God did this for me, so I know He can do something for you."

It not only raised her faith, but her faith became infectious. Africans who are in desperate circumstances will grasp at any straw that might improve their lot. Here was more than a straw, here was hope. God really does care about widows; Beatrice and her house were living proof of this. People's reaction, when they heard her testimony, was to jump from their seats to dance and shout praises to God for His faithfulness. Little did Beatrice realise it at the time, but this reaction of transferred faith was to ignite a mass movement that some people began to call, *"The mighty widows of Teso"*.

CHAPTER 13

The Calling of God

"For the gifts and the calling of God are irrevocable."
(Romans 11:29 NKJV)

When a husband dies in Africa, it is usually the case for the widow to go into obscurity. But God had not only called John Omese to the ministry, He had also called Beatrice. Surely God's calling doesn't die with the husband? God certainly had not finished with Beatrice. In fact, He had hardly begun.

Her first task was to visit all the local church pastors and encourage them. There was a serious possibility that now John had gone the ministry would collapse. Her message was simple but powerful:

"Despite the death of John this church will continue. If we give up we will be losers. Winners don't quit. We need to show the devil that even after John's death the Lord's work is still alive."

This was not an easy task for her. She was in deep mourning and heavily pregnant. Going round the bush churches is an arduous task at any time. She didn't have her own vehicle and had to rely on taxis and Mutatus.

Shortly after John's death, Beatrice heard about a widow's conference in Kampala organised by Ruth Birbwa. She had been told about it by a neighbour who had seen some publicity leaflets. She travelled alone on one of the overcrowded Mutatu minibus taxis. It was an uncomfortable journey that took about five hours. It was at this conference that God birthed in her the vision to begin a widows' ministry. On her return from Kampala she began to gather local widows for a prayer meeting in her father's already overcrowded house. With a broad smile on her face she says, "I inconvenienced everyone in my father's house with my widows."

Then the prayer meeting moved to the secretarial college which had a larger room.

Once Beatrice's own house was completed the prayer meetings moved there. Every room, the corridors and the veranda outside would be packed with widows calling out to God, day and night. A lady visiting from the UK donated 700,000 Shillings. This enabled them to pay six months rent on a small office. This served as the organisational centre and included another prayer room. Weekly prayer meetings from ten in the morning until four in the afternoon started. Once a month on Saturdays they prayed through the night. Thus the birth and the enduring character of the movement were established in prayer.

By August 2001, Beatrice realised it was time to hold their first widows' conference. She asked Pastor Matthew of the Soroti AOG church if she could use their hall for the widows and he agreed. She hired a large tent for the widows to sleep in. Invitations were sent out to local churches and everyone was invited to try to bring a little money to pay for the conference, or some food to share. The response to the financial appeal was very discouraging for Beatrice. At a pre-conference meeting with her friend Janet Esiku and other helpers, they realised that they only had 40,000 Shillings (£12) and Beatrice herself had donated 75% of that!

Several hundred excited widows arrived. The tent was not big enough to sleep the hundreds of widows, so they overflowed into the church at night. God moved powerfully in the meetings. Widows who were destitute cried out to God to meet them in their need as they prayed into the night. Beatrice began her powerful preaching and teaching ministry. The joy of worshipping together lifted their spirits. Laughing, singing and dancing characterised the lengthy times of worship. The awful sense of loneliness and rejection that most of them experienced was driven away with the love and fellowship they shared. Both in the meetings and over meals they shared their stories with each other. Many of them had horror stories of death and suffering at the hands of the LRA or Karamajong. Some had lost their children as well as their husbands. Others told how their children had been abducted and they often didn't know if they were still alive or suffering at the brutal hands of their captors. These terrible experiences are traumatic in themselves, but if the widow also experiences loneliness and rejection, she descends into utter hopelessness and depression.

There were many tears shed that weekend as they listened sympathetically to each other and prayed together. Yet the tears and the telling of the horrors and suffering were a kind of therapy. Here were others who had also suffered – people who didn't avoid them for fear they would have to listen to their problems. Incredibly, the powerful presence of God was able to lift them out of tears and into joy, at least for this blessed time. The most powerful praise that can be offered to God in this world is the praise that rises in spite of pain and destitution. Oh, they cared for each other, but best of all, they touched God who knew about their pain and cared. They touched eternity and knew that their abiding city was not of this world. A better day was coming.

Africans are socially minded people. They are family and community orientated. Unlike Westerners, they do not demand their privacy. In the West we are task orientated, we like to get the job done. It has often been said to me by Africans and even friends in Eastern Europe, "Please come and stay with us for a longer time."

The Westerner's reaction to this kind of invitation is to ask, "What will we *do*, while we are here?" The incomprehensible answer they will often get is, "Just come and be with us."

For the African the aim is often to just spend time together rather than have a task to accomplish. To them this is of great value and a sign of your care and friendship that someone is prepared to spend time with them in this way. Only by appreciating this aspect of the African culture can we begin to see how valuable Beatrice's ministry was – even before she was able to do anything in a practical or economic way for the widows. They were together. They had experienced similar ordeals. They were no longer totally isolated: they had friends who were interested in them when no one else was willing to be.

Other widows were the victims of AIDS. Sickness passed on from their now dead husbands would exact its morbid toll of pain and eventual death – sometimes on their children too. Their number included grandmothers, left alone to care for their dead children's orphans. It seemed as though the whole sorrowful spread of Africa's suffering was encapsulated in the experience of these women. Their gathering had become a microcosm of the phrase in the inscription on David Livingstone's tomb in Westminster Abbey: "...*this festering sore of the world.*" For those without the Gospel of Jesus Christ in Africa, not too much has changed. Poverty, oppression, illness, suffering and premature death are rampant.

Their faith was strengthened as they listened to testimonies and the preaching of God's Word. They sensed that they now had a voice in the community. In Beatrice they also had a spokesperson who was bold enough to be their advocate to the authorities. By the time the weekend was over, the widows returned to their homes, however poor they were, with a new hope in their hearts and even a spring in their step.

The plan was to have a main conference once a year and smaller gatherings in the villages. As things turned out, the number of large conferences proliferated to six or seven in a year, such was the demand.

One of the early widows' gatherings stands out as a pivotal moment in the development of the ministry. It was in a rural village, deep in the bush. It was difficult to get to and largely cut off from the town. Here the poverty and suffering was more acute. Some widows had very little shelter. They made a rough shack of leaves and sheets of plastic if they could find them. At night they lay on the damp ground and if it rained they spent a miserable cold and wet night. Their health suffered as a result and eventually they would inevitably die a painful death.

As Beatrice viewed her assembled widows she was moved by their obvious poverty. They looked older than their years and some were very sick. As usual, they responded to her visit and praised God heartily.

Beatrice sang and prayed with them but she felt a deep ache inside her. She was overcome with a sense of helplessness. They needed more than she could give them. They needed practical help. Their need was for food, shelter and warm clothing. Above all they needed a means to stay alive and live their allotted span in reasonable conditions.

Eventually, the obvious fact that she had nothing to give them became a deep cry to God and a burden she couldn't bear. She could hardly stop crying. They all had tears in abundance as they shared their woes. If God wanted her to do this work, He had to find a way for her to help them materially as well as spiritually. Unable to sleep that night she followed her accustomed habit and went out to pray. As she walked and cried out to God, the answer came. She didn't really understand what God meant or what it would entail. All she knew was God had spoken to her more powerfully than ever before and she must share it with the widows. Not just these widows, but every time she gathered with any group, she would share this prophetic word.

The next day as they gathered to worship, she shared with them the exact word God had given her: "Today is the last day that we cry – from now on we work! Being a widow is not a physical handicap, we will use our hands and work."

How to respond to the word, she wasn't sure. The only thing they knew how to do was to grow crops, so that is how they would begin. Whatever bit of land they could use, they would cultivate. She would ask God for land. She would ask anyone she could for land. They would begin small and expand as they could; a widows' cooperative would be born. This was going to add a whole new dimension to the widows' movement – working instead of crying. It may seem an obvious thing to do in hindsight, but it was a new idea. Widows just didn't do this sort of thing. They only faded away, with no status and no voice in the community. But then again, widows didn't have houses built for them either. Beatrice often says that everything went back to the provision of the house and the faith that it gave her.

Early in 2002, President Museveni and his wife Janet, who is a keen Christian, visited Soroti. It is the President's habit to visit the major towns of his country as often as he can to encourage everyone and see how things are progressing. Soroti was of special importance because it was the front line in the conflict with the LRA. Beatrice, representing the widows of the district, requested an audience with the President. Their request was one of many and there was no guarantee that they would be among those seen. Some people request to see the President for years. It is perfectly natural that a great number of people would like to see the President. She asked the officials to pass on a message to him, that the widows had been praying for the nation and that they would like to see the President, to bring a genuine word of appreciation for his work and to explain their predicament. Their request was granted.

The meeting was held in a specially erected tent beside State House, the President's official residence in that part of the country. For a whole week he held meetings with the officials of the town, tribal elders, business leaders, local police and security officers. Beatrice wrote a proposal for a scheme to help the widows and requested some help. The idea came to her during one of their many prayer meetings in town. The document began by thanking the President for two important achievements. First, greater security had come to their district – a direct result of his decision to appoint Mr. Musa and allow the reforming of the Arrow Boys. Secondly the provision of free primary school education for the first time in Uganda.

The President had personally visited the World Bank in New York to obtain help for this. The standard of this free education was still developing. Classes sometimes numbered as many two hundred children. People who could afford it still preferred to pay for the private schools. But for the widows, any education for their children was considered wonderful. The document went on to tell the President that they had begun their own savings and credit association to help widows out of their dire poverty. Their request for help was made in an African way. They asked the President to become a member and saver in their bank.

Beatrice was nervous, but trusting in God when the big moment came. She entered with her delegation of thirty widows and a copy of their proposal. They were sharing the proceedings with youth leaders and a group of their members. The youth were allowed to go first. When the widows' turn came, first they presented some symbolic gifts to the President. This was an echo of the ancient tradition of not approaching the chief without some gift for him. They presented three items: a traditional village chair, a hat and a shepherd's rod.

Beatrice explained to the President that she had had a dream in which the President had come to visit her in her home. She also explained that as she thought about the dream afterwards, the Lord had reminded her of the Bible passage about David as a young shepherd boy who was then called to shepherd God's people Israel. She told him that whenever he sat on this chair and held the rod he would be reminded of God's call on his life. Once he had been a fighter in the bush, struggling to bring liberation to his people. Now he was a shepherd to his people and whenever he sat on this chair, God would give him a revelation. President Museveni and his wife were delighted.

The boldness of this unusual and personal prophetic message to him from a young woman must have impressed the President and his wife. He was both moved and amused. He took the rod, put on the hat and sat on the chair. Local journalists and Presidential officials immediately took the opportunity to photograph the moment. The next day, the pictures appeared in the newspapers. As he sat on the chair the President asked Beatrice what else she was involved in. She explained that she used to be a teacher, but now she was full-time in this widows' ministry. He was very pleased to hear this and told her that he thought it was an excellent thing to be doing.

Her friend Pauline read out the proposal to the entourage assembled before the President. Then Beatrice led some prayers for the nation with her widows enthusiastically joining in. With a broad smile on his face and a note of humour in his voice, the President asked Beatrice, "Are you the Pastor of our meeting today?"

Reciprocating the mood of the moment, Beatrice smiled back and said, "Yes, I am."

There were smiles all round and the usual formality of such meetings was relaxed. Then the serious moment came for Beatrice to present her proposal. With God-given courage she faced the President and told him of the plight of widows in the district and how she planned, with a little help, to try to assist them. She emphasised that God had burdened her heart for the suffering of the widows.

The President was impressed with both the proposal and the bold manner with which it was presented. Just as important – or perhaps more important – his wife Janet was impressed. She appreciated the spiritual aspects of the ministry and was very enthusiastic to help. Subsequently, when the President visited Soroti, on several occasions he requested that Beatrice would come and report to him and his wife on the progress of the scheme. At times, Janet Museveni came to Soroti alone and visited the widows' group.

They waited with baited breath for the result of the interview. They were overjoyed to be told that the President had given them 20,000,000 Shillings (£6,000) and a small tractor. It was in two instalments. Ten million was given immediately and the balance a month later. Now Beatrice had something to work with. Again God was faithful to His word in answering her prayers. She consulted with her widows' committee and they decided to purchase a large plot of virgin bush land, which is the cheapest. It is cheap because it has to be cleared before anything can be grown on it. The clearing of such a large plot was a massive job.

Then they purchased a large number of goats for distribution to the widows. Every widow who received a goat had to produce kids from it and return one kid to the widows' association within a year, which almost all did. This enabled the goat scheme to be spread further each year.

The balance of Shillings was deposited in the Savings and Credit Society to finance future projects. Now the really hard work began. At this stage, Beatrice could have been forgiven for thinking that this was the answer to their prayers and they would slowly build up for this level. God however, had much larger plans for this ministry. This was only the beginning. God's call on her life was for something much bigger than she could ever have dreamed of. Her faith in God had remained steadfast though the early sufferings of the hazardous journey to Kaniki Bible College and childbirth in Zambia, through to the loss of her husband. In God's own economy these experiences would bear fruit a hundredfold.

The next time the President visited Soroti, about three months later, Beatrice and her vice chairperson, Janet, met with him again. This time they wanted to thank him for his help, give him another gift and report on the progress they had made. They presented their accounts which showed exactly how the money had been used. President Museveni said to her, "I want to thank you for the work you are doing and for coming here today. Most people do not come back to thank me, but come to demand more."

Beatrice then told the President that they were having a widows' conference the following week and they had invited "The First Lady" to join them. She asked him if his wife had received the invitation. He said that she hadn't, but she could come. She was told to give her cell phone number to one of the officials and they would confirm the following week the details of the First Lady's visit to the conference. Next week came and no confirmation had come. The conference began and still no word had been received. Beatrice was in the habit of handing her cell phone over to a friend while she spoke to the widows in case it rang. What she didn't realise was that an official was desperately trying to reach her, but the lady who held the phone switched it off every time it rang! The official eventually rang someone else to pass a message on to her. Finally the arrangement was made. The First Lady would attend the final day of the conference.

Beatrice panicked a little now. She had no idea how to receive the First Lady. At the two meetings with the President and in conversations afterwards, she had become acquainted with some of the government ministers who usually accompanied the President on these trips. She had even taken their cell phone numbers. She needed someone's help. She first rang the President's minister responsible for the district. He said he was in Kampala and unable to return immediately. She then called the Presidential Commissioner. He was also in Kampala and unable to assist. She called a third minister and received the same response.

A little desperate now, she finally phoned Hon. Grace Akelo, the Minister who represented the League of Women to the government. Her reply was, "I am in Moroto, but I am on my way back. I will be with you tomorrow and I will help. Meanwhile, go to the people who make the large banners and get them to make one overnight."

The banner makers rose to the task and overnight produced a large banner saying, *We welcome the First Lady to the Teso Widows' Prayer Conference*. It was erected at the entrance to the church. Then Grace Akelo suggested that the event should be moved to an hotel because the church was too small. Beatrice refused to do this, saying the First Lady must come to the church. Beatrice told her that the church had a large tent, but they didn't have the money to hire it. The Minister told her to hire the tent and she would bring the money to pay for it and the hire of the chairs.

That evening an advance team of soldiers arrived to set up security for the visit. This was the confirmation that she was coming. The next morning it was announced on the radio that the First Lady would be visiting the Widows' Conference in Soroti. Everyone in the town was amazed. Soroti buzzed with the news. Soldiers with sniffer dogs searched everywhere and the whole town was tight with security. Grace Akelo arrived in her ministerial car and quickly organised a delegation of officials from the town to meet the First Lady at the Flying School airfield at the appointed time. Beatrice, who at this stage didn't have a vehicle, found herself seated next to Grace Akelo in the back of the ministerial car as they drove out to the Flying School to await the Presidential helicopter that was bringing in the First Lady.

As they transported Janet Museveni back to town, Beatrice sat in the back of the car, shoulder to shoulder with a Government Minister and the First Lady, chatting away as if they were old friends. Sitting between these two very important people, the thought that she was still a poor widow wondering how to pay the bills didn't cross her mind. God was providing for her, now He was about to provide for her widows too.

More than eight hundred excited widows, and about two hundred gate-crashers wanting to see the First Lady, crammed into the tent. The noise that greeted the arrival of the First Lady was deafening. Pastor Omagro from the church opened the final day's meetings with prayer. Then Beatrice stood up and welcomed the First Lady to the conference. She then welcomed the mayor of Soroti and called on him to introduce the various local government officials who had all hurriedly changed their plans for that day and arrived in their best suits as though they had been planning it for months! Beatrice then gave a speech and welcomed the Minister Grace Akelo. The Minister gave a short speech and also welcomed the First Lady who was the main speaker of the day.

The First Lady's speech was in fact a sermon, full of encouragement for the widows. From the book of Exodus she read verses about the Children of Israel who were in captivity. She made the point that although they were suffering, God had not forgotten them. She compared this with their situation and assured them that God had not forgotten them. She said that it was important for them to have training in entrepreneurship. She even offered to arrange some training for them. This was a promise that she kept. The worship was even more exuberant than usual. The atmosphere was electric. The downtrodden widows now had a voice and an advocate, in the President's wife, at the very highest level in the land.

Suddenly, the widows association and Beatrice herself were important people. This was, of course, in stark contrast to the way widows were normally regarded. God had reversed the situation. Now they were regarded with some admiration, the reputation of *the mighty widows of Teso* was growing.

The President and his wife became fans of the Teso Widows Entrepreneurial Association and began talking about them all over Uganda. They were held up as an example of self-help and success if you were prepared to work hard. The President's wife would also add that faith in God was just as important and the President would agree. President Museveni had been working hard to combat the age old tradition of corruption and this was an example of transparency that impressed him. Peter and Clara Marie Pedersen, back in Kaniki Bible College, would have been very proud of her.

CHAPTER 14

God's Answer

After the meetings with the President and the First Lady, God moved in an amazing way to transform the widows' ministry and lift it to a much higher level than anyone could have dreamt of. The President and his wife were now talking about the widows wherever they went. They wanted others to emulate them. If poor widows could make a success of their lives, others could too. The endemic African problems of poverty, lack of opportunity and corruption could be overcome if you had determination, a work ethic, and faith in God.

Pastor Franklin was a chaplain in the army. He heard about the widows of Soroti in a meeting he attended where the President was speaking. Pastor Franklin subsequently came to Soroti for some different meetings and decided to try to meet some of these now famous widows. He enquired of the leaders of the meetings he was attending and they directed him to Beatrice. She explained to him that he was not the first to come and ask about the widows' work, but that most people only wanted to see the ones who live in Soroti. This is more convenient for them. However, she explained that the widows with the most desperate need live in the villages and if he really wanted to see the true picture, he would need to travel into the bush with her and see for himself. He agreed that these were the ones he should visit and as he had a vehicle they could go together. They visited some bush villages, testing Pastor Franklin's vehicle to its limits over the rough bush roads. He was very moved when he saw the plight of these destitute women. He was glad he had made the effort to reach these villages.

He wanted to help, but didn't really know how. He asked Beatrice to write a memo detailing the condition and needs of the Teso widows which he could refer to if he should meet anyone who might help them. He asked her to bring the memo to the lodge where he was staying the next morning.

That evening, back in the guest lodge in town where he was staying, Franklin was in conversation with other guests in the lodge. One of them was the Director and founder of a well-funded American NGO working in Uganda. He was in town, at the invitation of another Pastor, to research the need to build a youth centre in the town. He had originally come to Uganda to help some of the many orphans in the land. As several guests sat round relaxing at the end of their busy day, each talked about the reasons they were in Soroti at that time. Pastor Franklin took the opportunity to relate his story of hearing about the Soroti widows from the President and that he had met Beatrice their leader, sharing how moved he was to see the appalling conditions and the suffering of these women.

The following morning, Beatrice went to the lodge with her memo for Pastor Franklin. She arrived later than planned and the guests were already checking out. She saw Pastor Franklin and handed him the memo. The NGO Director was also checking out and Pastor Franklin called him over to introduce Beatrice, explaining that this was the lady he had been talking about who had so impressed him. He handed him the memo and told him that it was an explanation of the needs of the widows. Having read the memo, the Director asked Beatrice for her cell phone number and email address.

Shortly after this, Beatrice went to Kampala to a college where she had enrolled to study Theology part time. She was attempting to catch up on the studies she had missed at Kaniki. While there, she had a call from this NGO Director asking her if she had received an email he had sent. She explained that she hadn't because she was not at home, but in Kampala. He was also in Kampala and so they agreed to meet.

He asked Beatrice to explain her vision for the widows' ministry. She expanded on the information in the memo. She gave him a detailed account of the hopeless condition of these widows and their children. She wanted to relieve their suffering. Moreover, she wanted the relief to be sustainable not temporary. She didn't want to feed the widows for a few days, but to enable them to fend for themselves long term. There is an old saying, often quoted by aid workers: "Give me a fish and you feed me for a day; teach me to fish and you feed me for life."

Having listened to Beatrice, the Director then asked an important question – a question that is so often not asked in these circumstances. He asked what the greatest needs were in the work with the widows. So often, Western organisations and churches assume that they are the ones that know best the needs in situations and how to help. They often fail to consult the local people who have the best knowledge of the problems and what is the best solution. A patronising attitude and even cultural arrogance are unfortunately all too common. There is also often an element of *he who pays the piper calls the tune.*

This NGO was different. They genuinely wanted Beatrice's view of the needs of the widows. She told the Director that their greatest need was for transport. What little help they had for the widows was very difficult, time consuming and expensive to deliver by public transport. The Director understood that step one had to be some vehicles if anything else was to be done. He asked what else they needed. Food and lots of it was the answer. Most of the widows were malnourished or even starving. Many were dying painful premature deaths due to malnourishment. The Director said he would organise the food.

What Beatrice didn't realise at this point was that this NGO had enough resources available to make a real difference in the situation. Beatrice soon had three vehicles available and tons of food being delivered. Once again God was answering prayer and keeping His word to Beatrice. The chain of people and events that began with Paul and Tessa, included the President and his wife, then Pastor Franklin, had led to this provision through the NGO. What began as a word from

God and a spark of faith was now growing into a ministry that was making a difference in the lives of many. Much more was to come.

It is one thing to talk or to promise, it is another to deliver. The first practical outcome of this conversation was the Director's second visit to Soroti. He arrived in a pick-up truck filled with food. The word spread like wildfire and within minutes many excited widows gathered to greet the Director. There was lots of noise and praising God. The food was distributed and he left the vehicle behind for the use of the ministry. For the widows, this was the first real sign that it was not just talk; things were happening. Unfortunately, Westerners have a reputation for going to Africa and making enthusiastic promises in the excitement of the moment that are forgotten when they return home. In Africa, centuries of deprivation has produced a culture that always hopes things will get better. It has been said that "without hope you die". One result of this is when an African asks for help from a Westerner, they are usually too embarrassed to say "no" so they say things such as, "I will think about it" or even "I will pray about it." They don't realise that to the ever hopeful African, any answer except "no" means "yes."

Beatrice knew that this provision was only an emergency measure. The widows needed a means of fending for themselves and access to medical treatment. She now had vehicles to get to the villages and the IDP camps, but she would never be able to visit the hundreds of villages where the widows lived and, for the most part, were prisoners of their environment. She needed to train leaders for each village and more leaders over those for each district. She needed to both inspire faith in them and, in practical ways, give them the means to produce food.

She needed to get the widows together and choose leaders to be trained and inspired. So the next time the Director asked her what she needed now, she explained that she needed a conference centre – a big one! I know of no other NGO that would have responded positively to that request. They simply would not have seen it as a priority or even the need for it. Again, this Director was different. He was experienced in the building trade and he knew exactly what was needed and where to get it from.

In the warehousing trade they are simply called "Big Sheds". Just tell the right company what capacity you need and a computer will design it for you and include a list of materials. Within a remarkably short space of time, Beatrice's conference centre was flat-packed, on a ship sailing from the USA and bound for the port of Mombasa on the coast of Kenya. The Director was waiting in Soroti for it to arrive. His building trade experience meant he had the knowledge of how to supervise its construction. When the structure was complete, it would hold two thousand widows. A small hall for leaders' meetings was also built adjacent to the large hall. The site was fenced and landscaped. This was now the largest auditorium in the northern half of Uganda.

If anyone had questioned the usefulness of a Big Shed for this ministry, they could now observe that it had become the central organising facility where the widows could gather for worship, teaching and instruction in how to organise the widows in their area. Coming together in this way had a galvanising effect on the widows. They returned home from the conferences with their faith raised and a conviction in their hearts that things really could improve for them. They were no longer condemned to a lingering death from malnutrition, shunned by their communities because they were helpless widows whose problems were so profound that no one could help and therefore didn't want to hear about them.

After the initial emergency relief it was time to experiment and see if the vision could be turned into reality. They distributed packages of seeds to their first group of widows – seeds for maize, ground nuts, beans and cassava stems. They were given on the understanding that when their crops had grown, they would return the same quantity of seed to the widows' ministry for distribution to other widows. The extra seeds could be used again for their next crop. Their second crop would be more profitable because they had repaid their seed "loan". They did the same with a hundred cows. The five district leaders were given cows first. Then others who they recommended as trustworthy and in dire need were also given cows. Anyone who received a cow had to return a calf within a year and their loan was repaid. The same method was applied to hundreds of goats.

Their success rate was amazing. Hardly any of the widows failed to repay their "loan". Such schemes have often been tried in Africa under various names such as "micro-credit schemes". When they are run well with experienced managers who know the local markets, they can be successful. The added dimension with Beatrice's widows was the spiritual one. The widows understood that the motivation behind it all was a mission to help them in both practical and spiritual ways. The NGO was naturally curious to see if this would work. The Director had wisely put his faith in good local people such as Beatrice and acted according to their requests. He and some of his colleagues attended the next widows' conference. Several thousand turned up. It was a happy and chaotic time of enthusiastic worship and trying to feed and sleep the numbers that came from all over Teso. The Director took the opportunity to ask the assembled widows to raise their hands if they had received seeds. He did the same for the goats and the cows. The response he saw convinced him that the scheme was working. Within about three years of the commencement of this project, Beatrice had over fifteen thousand widows who had joined and were benefiting from the ministry

Alongside the successful micro-schemes, Beatrice wanted to try some larger projects to finance the expansion of the ministry. They would need to replace the vehicles, pay for servicing and repairs. The office and administration needed to be sustainable. They began the enormous, back-breaking task of clearing the large plot of land that they had purchased with money from the President. The land was primeval bush; nothing had ever been planted there since the Genesis flood. Cutting the grass, digging out bushes and even small trees was hard work under the merciless African sun. When they needed to, they called in specialist teams of men who earned a living by removing larger trees from land marked out for agriculture. This was all financed by the NGO. They also helped by purchasing four bulls for the ploughing. Some people might be critical and say that this is not good for the environment. If you say this to an African, he might tell you that your environmental "issue" is his solution to the daily task of feeding himself and his family!

The plan for the land was to use it to produce cash crops. They planted 50,000 pineapple suckers and in between the rows of pineapples they planted several hundred orange trees. These would give their first crop in three years. This was virgin land and the crop is totally organic. The result was the biggest, juiciest, sweetest pineapples you can imagine! The pineapples cover an area of about twelve acres. Whenever they needed technical advice, they called on Joseph who was a government Agricultural Officer. He is also a faithful Christian and a prominent member of his local AOG church. He has been an enormous help to the whole project.

The NGO Director just kept on asking that question: "What else do you need?"

The widows who had a family plot and the physical strength to cultivate it were now beginning to prosper. They were also gaining respect from their neighbours. People were no longer afraid to speak to them. They could engage in happy conversations about the widows' project and their part in it. In Soroti it was literally "the talk of the town". They could proudly display their cow, calf, goats and crops. People would even buy produce from them if they had some to spare. The benefits were manifold, both practically and spiritually.

But what about the widows who were too old, too sick and too weak to hoe, weed and carry water to their plots? These were still suffering and dying painful deaths. The food they had been given had run out. Who would care for them? Beatrice discussed with the NGO the idea of building a hospice. She wanted a comfortable and happy place where the oldest and the terminally ill widows could live out their final days on earth in a Christian community where their physical needs could be met.

Once again, this NGO rose to the challenge. Plans were drawn up, permissions applied for and building began on the hospice. This was a big undertaking. It would need professional staff and lots of equipment. Within a year, the first widows were moving in. Some had to be carried in on stretchers from their villages. Some seemed hardly alive, just a bag of skin and bone. Regular food, shelter from the weather and medical attention had a remarkable effect on some of these older widows. As with a hospice in the West, the anticipation was that anyone entering the hospice was making a one-way journey; they were there to die peacefully.

However, some of the widows began to put on a little weight. Their health began to return. There weren't all that old after all. They had just looked old because they were sick and starving. Soon some wanted those seeds and a cow so that they could go home to their village and care for themselves. Some wanted to see their neighbours. There may even have been an element of, "Ha! You thought I was finished, but I'm not! I'll show you that I can make a go of things, I just needed a little help." For some of them, after years of rejection, struggle and suffering, to be able to walk proudly through their ancestral village with their head held high was more empowering than most of us could imagine.

About half of those that had come to die began to realise that it was not their time to die, and with their new health and strength could resume the life that dire circumstances had robbed them of. A few were strong enough to return to their village, but enjoyed life in the hospice so much they just didn't want to go home. Perhaps for some of them, the memory of their suffering was just too much; they didn't want to risk moving out. Most of the widows in the hospice would gather each morning in the chapel for a devotional time of singing and prayer. Someone would share a word from the Bible and the widows themselves were keen to share their testimony of how God had blessed them and met their needs.

Widows at the conference centre

Some of her leaders outside the widows conference centre

Typical leaders' conference at the centre

CHAPTER 15

Victory Over the Darkness

Mr. Musa and his Arrow Boys, working with the UPLA and empowered by the faith and prayer of the churches in Teso, had driven the LRA out of their homelands. This didn't immediately help the other areas further north. They were still held in the LRA's grip of fear. However, Teso had shown the way to defeat the insurgents and the solution was spiritual. The soldiers and officers of the Ugandan People's Defence Force had shown great courage and commitment, only to be frustrated by the evil powers that controlled Kony and his thugs. Their training and equipment was far superior to the rebels and if they could only engage them in open battle, they could easily defeat the enemy. They searched the region for the LRA, following up reports of their activities and camp sites. However, when they arrived, the LRA was always gone. Evidence of their stay was tragically plentiful, but most of the time the rebels themselves had been warned by the spirits and they moved on.

Mr Musa Ecweru - Made regional governor of Teso by the President, then raised up the 'Arrow Boys' militia that drove the LRA out of Teso. Now a Cabinet Minister responsible for disaster planning

Former rebel commander Kenneth Banya told how spirit voices would speak to them and warn them of the number of the government forces and the direction from which they were coming. Kony's prophetic powers greatly enhanced his mystique with his men. Eye witnesses tell how the rebel camps were set out in mystic patterns and symbols. Special rites, blood covenants, charms, chants, drugs, incantations, ritual cannibalism, snakes, "sacred" water and drumming were all employed to bring down the spirits to possess Kony and his people. Kony himself reported to a council of seven spirits. The LRA leadership gave themselves to the spirits and invited them in. They committed themselves to the same age-old deal of blood in exchange for power. Many people ask how humans can be so inhuman to others. Throughout human history there have been those willing to engage in these evil covenants and this, at least in part, explains how such atrocities can occur.

The activities of Kony and the LRA were all the more obscene because they proclaimed that they were doing it in God's name. Everything had a quasi-religious element. Abductees were immediately "anointed" with the sacred water. They were told that the water had cleansed them from all sin. They were told that sacred oil could heal them from any disease. Then various parts of their body were anointed with a mixture of white powder and oil in the form of white crosses. They were told not to wash these off for three days. The abductees were now ready to hear from the spirits and Kony would be the mouthpiece. He would stand before them and go into a trance, his eyes would change and his head slump, he would speak in a voice that clearly was not his own. Those listening would not remember much of what was said, but a spirit-appointed scribe would be given the power to write down everything that had been said – nothing was to be forgotten. The demonic spirits rarely had such a grip on a man and they were determined to make the most of the opportunity.

He frequented special sites to which he needed to return every six months as he felt his power diminishing. Most important among these were Awere Hill and Kilak Hills. In these places he would commune with powerful spirits that resided there and his power would be renewed. As the spirit power diminished he would become friendlier and laugh and joke with his men. But when the spirits' power was renewed in him he became unpredictable and dangerous. He killed at least twenty-eight of his own children and three of his wives as blood offerings. No one could oppose him. Anyone who dared to disagree with him was severely dealt with. One of his Captains, Ray Apere, who later became a Christian, once openly argued with him.

"You are killing my own people. Why do we kill our own?"

Kony was so angry that he immediately ordered his officer to be killed. Another commander interceded for him and the punishment was reduced to three hundred strokes with a rod on his body. The beating was so severe it was almost fatal and the officer was still bleeding weeks later. The abductees suffered a lot. Long, barefoot forced marches through the bush caused horrendous, painful damage to their feet. They were not fed properly and often lived on roots and drank dirty water and their own urine.

It seemed at one stage that the rebels could do what they liked, attack anywhere. Some even feared that they would take over the country. People knew their power was demonic and they wondered how it could ever be stopped. Vehicles were brazenly stopped on the road and burned – sometimes with the owners still in them. Many buses were burned, making people afraid to travel. The northern part of the country was totally disrupted and fear fell on everyone. Throughout the whole of northern Uganda normal life ceased. Crops were not raised, schools, hospitals, clinics, shops and public transport were closed down. Normal law enforcement and local government ceased to function in many places. More than half a million people fled their homes. The LRA became paranoid about bicycles. They were regarded as instruments of their enemies. Information about the location of LRA forces could be, and often was, carried to the authorities by people on bicycles. Anyone found riding a bicycle was killed or had their feet hacked off.

For twenty years the suffering in northern Uganda was ignored by the rest of the world. A United Nations spokesman described it as "a moral outrage". There is a whole generation that has not known peace, growing to adulthood knowing only fear and disruption. In the camps they have no education or adequate healthcare. Poverty and emotional trauma is their experience for years. People sink into moral corruption, sexual depravity and crime. They have little faith in God and turn to the very witchcraft that put them there. They have lost their homes, businesses and livelihood. Many are handicapped with bullet or machete wounds or lost limbs. Many have succumbed to sheer hopelessness and depression, causing the suicide rate to soar. Even the southern part of Uganda ignored what was happening in the north. Their attitude was: *We have suffered so much from those northern people under Idi Amin and Obote, now their children are killing their own people. It is not our business that Acholi kill Acholi.*

Even the churches and Christian leaders failed to speak out or act. If there was going to be a final victory over this darkness, something spiritual and more powerful than the evil forces that strode across the land needed to be employed.

Providentially, God began to move among the churches in the southern parts of Uganda. They recognised that their country north of the Nile was under the control of evil. The Spirit of God began to rise up within the churches, bringing a strong conviction that something should, and more importantly, could be done about the situation. Suddenly they became acutely aware of the bloodshed and the long history of idolatry; that the land of the Acholi was crying out for deliverance. The Spirit of God spoke a prophetic word and told them to declare war on witchcraft and idolatry. The response of the churches was nights of prayer and fasting. They knew this was the only way to unlock the situation and bring the power of God to bear.

Then came what appeared to be the first breakthrough – the Sudanese government finally accepted the Ugandan President's demand to open their borders and allow the UPDF to pursue Kony's army into

Sudan which had been their safe haven. Operation "Iron Fist" was swift and relentless. The LRA were taken by surprise. Ten thousand UPLA troops crossed into Sudan in pursuit of the LRA. After some initial success, the LRA once again just melted away into the bush. Three months later the LRA were back, angry and determined to have their revenge. The angry backlash and atrocities became more savage and evil than ever. Nowhere was safe in Gulu district. More children were abducted, more women raped and abducted or just horrendously mutilated. Hundreds of civilians were murdered. The battle was not yet over, but it was a beginning. The churches and their leadership realised that the answer to this intractable horror lay with them and their God.

One of the leading intercessors, Brigadier General David Wakaalo, serving as Chaplain of the UPDF was given a vision in which he saw the Acholi district covered in blood. He saw that the vision of blood represented a powerful spirit of death hovering over the district. It is natural for an army officer to believe that an inferior enemy could be defeated by his forces. The vision, however, revealed to him that the enemy would never be defeated by military means alone. The answer had to be spiritual warfare. This led to a series of meetings between key church, military and government leaders. "Operation Gideon" was born. Leading Pastors Julius Oyet, James Magara and Mike Kimuli mobilised the whole nation to pray and fast for a month in preparation for "Redeeming the nation". Church leaders from the south, west and central Uganda mobilised to courageously travel to the north to pray in the most dangerous areas. This was of great significance. In many ways it was an act of forgiveness. The prevailing attitude – *that the north are getting what they deserve* – had to be eradicated.

Many pastors were justifiably afraid to join the group. Just going there in defiance of LRA threats, was in itself, an act of spiritual warfare. The satanic fear that gripped the area was being seriously challenged by these amazing men and women of God. Everyone closely examined their lives, repenting before God, before they dared to join this life-threatening journey.

Their first event was a mass rally in the Pece stadium, the largest in Gulu town. In spite of the threats from the rebels and temperatures of over forty degrees, thousands packed the stadium far beyond its safe capacity and thousands more were outside, such was the longing for deliverance. Acholi evangelist, Julius Oyet preached powerfully to the gathered masses. Going straight to the heart of the problem, he outlined the history of witchcraft and idolatry in their area. The hearts of the people were moved to a deep repentance. Thousands began to move towards the podium, removing fetishes and symbols of witchcraft from their bodies and throwing them on the platform. These symbols of witchcraft power are purchased from the witchdoctors, sometimes at great cost. The more you pay for it, the more powerful it will be! Many Africans wear or carry these items to ward off the effects of evil spirits or to appease their ancestral spirits. As they pushed their way to the podium, many were crying out in a loud voice, "Jesus, we need you. Jesus, please help us."

Some did more than this. They revealed the highly secret locations of sacred witchcraft sites and altars in the region. Julius called out the different clans. One by one, with their leaders, they came forward to repent. Powerful principalities and powers of darkness that had stood proud and unchallenged for many generations were being torn down. This was the great turning point.

Satan could do nothing about this. He is powerless in the face of godly repentance and people rejecting the bonds in which he has held them. Thousands gave their lives to the Lord. Numerous backsliders repented and turned again to God. Revival is a word used for many things in these days, but this was surely worthy of that description.

President Museveni was in Gulu at the time, personally directing his troops in their operations against the LRA. It didn't take long before some of his officers began to report what was happening across town. As a result of this, Julius Oyet was called to a meeting with the President and asked to make a presentation. He later told how the President said to him,

"You did in a weekend what we couldn't do in months."

It was obvious to those present that many of the things that the President heard came as a surprise to him. The importance of what he was hearing was not lost on President Museveni. Perhaps for the first time, he began to see for himself the spiritual nature of the conflict. Part way through the briefing, he interrupted Julius Oyet and called into the meeting his senior military commanders. President Museveni's top military men listened in silence to the briefing. One of the most interested listeners was Gen. Aronda Nyakairima, the Supreme Commander of the UPDF. He was not expecting to hear about spiritual things. Eventually, he began to see the connection between what Juilus Oyet was saying and the difficulties the military were facing. Before the briefing was finished, President Museveni called a halt to it and simply asked the evangelist, "What do we need to do?" He had heard enough to convince him that these men and women of God had the key that might unlock the situation.

After some prayer, it was decided that the military would transport groups of selected believers to each LRA altar site. Military helicopters and armed convoys were used where necessary. It was a very dangerous trip for each of the groups. The believers were to destroy each site and altar in the name of the Lord. This would have been considered far too dangerous by the general Acholi population. To attempt this was certain death – not from the LRA, but from the spirits. Most of the LRA themselves would not dare to enter these sites. It was only Kony and a few of his most powerful elite that dared to enter. This was now an historical and strategic alliance between the government, the military and the Church. Everyone realised that the Church was the key.

Kony soon knew about this because the spirits informed him that people were going to pray at the sacred sites in an attempt to destroy him. His reaction was arrogant: "Let them try, we will see what happens."

The first place visited was Awere Hill, the most important site for Kony. This was the place where he received his power and was the source of his precious and powerful "sacred water". Only he dared to climb this rock and collect the water. For others to attempt this meant death, such was the evil power of this place. When the soldiers arrived, they were reluctant to go near. Three times they were ordered to climb the rock, but they refused. They would rather face military punishment than risk touching the rock. One officer led the way and began to climb. He died immediately.

Thus it was in March 2003 that a group of godly men, in an awesome display of faith and courage, defied the powers of hell and began to climb Awere Hill. Operation Gideon was under way. The men of God climbed to the top unharmed. Then they all held hands and cried out in a loud voice, "The Lord is God, the Lord is God."

Then, in prayer, they reclaimed the rock in the Name of their God who had created it. Their first task was to tackle the rock pool containing Kony's sacred and immensely powerful water. In a bold challenge to Kony's most powerful spirit, they made scoops from leaves and scooped out the water from the pool until it was drained. It simply ran down the sun baked rocks and evaporated. None of them died or suffered any ill effects – the power was broken. The soldiers who stood a safe distance from the rock observed with astonishment. They began praying and raising their hands in worship, submitting their lives to the living God.

One of the other groups visiting another LRA worship site at Awach made a shocking discovery. As they destroyed the altar, they discovered beneath it the remains of a burned human body that had been sacrificed to the spirit of that place. They were overcome with grief that their people did this kind of thing. The leader of the group, falling to his knees, cried out in great anguish to God, confessing the sins of his people:

> "An Acholi man has done this. My fathers have done this. God, my fathers have done this. My parents have done this. Forgive us, O God."

Others in the group wept and cried to God to forgive their people. Such crimes would be devastating in any society, but in the African culture it was worse. Even the evil practitioners of witchcraft never usually did this to their own people. The powerful bonds of family, clan and tribe that are the backbone of African culture had been desecrated.

Another group needed to go by helicopter to reach the remote and important site in the Kilak Hills. This, more than any other site, was traditionally associated with the spirits that ruled the Acholi people. Once again there was a pool of deadly water. Nothing survived in it. Local people had observed that even a leaf blown into or over it by the wind, would instantly wither. This time the believers jumped into the water and even drank it. The accompanying soldiers were amazed at the power of God. They joined in the euphoric rejoicing. When challenged, all the soldiers gave their life to Christ and were baptised in the very water that they had been so afraid of. The awe inspiring accounts of this spread throughout Acholi like wildfire. The people knew the power of this water and the fear it had generated for centuries among their people. Only the most powerful sorcerers and witchcraft practitioners ever dared to enter this place.

Kony instantly felt his power draining away. Upon his capture, Kony's top aide Brig. Gen. Kenneth Banya, quoted the rebel leader as saying,: "The spirits have left me and it is all the fault of those Christians."

All the LRA sacred sites were being systematically destroyed. The destruction of the sites was followed up by prayer meetings all over the district. Kony called his commanders together and warned them that the spirits had left him and his power was gone. One eye witness recalled his words: "I have to inform you that today the spirits have left me and they will not come back."

Now the military campaign took on a new impetus. Now the UPLA was ambushing the LRA. Intelligence reports could be followed up and the LRA groups still there were easily defeated by the superior training and equipment of the UPDF. Kony and the remnant of his army were forced to flee back into Sudan. The UPDF followed them across the border. Camp after camp was destroyed. They eventually found the main LRA headquarters, a vast camp stocked with a massive pile of weapons and ammunition. Anyone foolish enough to stay and fight was destroyed and the equipment captured.

The rebels began leaving the bush and surrendering to the Ugandan authorities. Many of the women and children that had been abducted were now released to go home. Sadly, there were many who would never make that journey of hope, having died at the hands of Kony and his thugs or the appalling conditions in which they were forced to live.

People all over Acholi district heard the bombing and the attacks on the rebel camps. Parents whose children had been abducted cried out to God that their children would not be killed. One mother said, "I had the vision of bombs falling on my daughter and I was afraid."

Some even went to consult with their local witchdoctors in an attempt to protect their children. Some escapees from the LRA warned these parents against this. They told them that if they did this, their children would surely die because the level of witchcraft practiced by Kony was so powerful, only prayers to the living God could protect them.

In contrast to this, those who had steadfastly trusted only in God with prayer and fasting were now seeing results. Women and children lost in the bush with the LRA for years were emerging and returning to their families in their thousands. Many were severely traumatised, particularly the children. Many of the girls had become wives and mothers. The boys were in a worse state. Forced to commit unspeakable atrocities, they lived in a world of nightmares, flashbacks and often warped personalities. Most would never know what they could and should have been. This was a lost generation of Acholi boys and teenagers. Some of the abductees were Christians; many of them testified to how God kept them alive against all the odds.

As the autumn of 2004 approached, the Acholi district began to come back to life. Vehicles were again seen on the roads. People returned to their plots of land and built huts and houses. Businesses were resumed and churches reopened. New churches began to spring up. Many former rebels repented and gave their lives to Christ. Even some former witchdoctors and sorcerers repented and were born again. Amazing evangelistic crusades were held in the Gulu stadium. Many came to Christ and the blind, lame and crippled were restored to health. God was present in power to save and heal.

Sadly, tens of thousands of the internally displaced people would remain in the squalid camps for years to come. These are the destitute ones with no money, no land, no home and no hope. Their scars will remain for some time to come until the government and aid agencies can resettle them back in their homeland. Some will die in the camps from AIDS or other diseases. Some will die of a broken heart.

CHAPTER 16

Epilogues

The Aboke Girls

God had not forgotten the Aboke Girls. Their parents made sure that the campaign and publicity continued to bring them to the attention of their government, international opinion and the United Nations. Little did the LRA realise who they had taken on when they abducted the girls from St Mary's College. Janet Akelo, one of the Aboke Girls, testified that through her many years of suffering at the hands of the LRA and all the horrors and deaths she had witnessed, her faith in God remained unwavering. She never went to sleep without communing with God. The gentle sounds of the African night mingled with her whispered prayers. She often told God that she knew He was constantly watching over her. The girls were forbidden to pray together. It was in the dark, still hours of the night and in their dreams that God came to them and connected them with the prayers of their families. At one stage, angry at the media attention about the Aboke Girls, they were sentenced to death by the LRA. But fearful of the worldwide repercussions, this was commuted to two hundred strokes of the cane – a punishment so severe that it could be fatal. This punishment often left their young bodies badly scarred for life. They were left lying unconscious on the ground. One girl was finished off by being brutally beaten with rocks until she died. She cried out to her friend, "Grace, please help me." These were her dying words. Sadly, not all the Aboke Girls came home.

Florence Lako often had dreams about her daughter Angela. This way she knew Angela was still alive. One night she had a vivid dream about Angela. She woke up and prayed for the rest of the night and she knew there had been a spiritual breakthrough. That summer, the determined pursuit by the UPDF seriously disrupted the discipline and tight security of the LRA. Many of the Aboke Girls who were still alive began to escape or to be released.

On the night of July 19th 2004, Charlotte Awino, after eight long years of captivity, had a dream. The Lord came to her and told her, *"Today you will go home, today you will see your people."* She wondered how this could be. It was impossible for her to escape. Charlotte was considered by the LRA as one of the leaders among the Aboke Girls. She was very closely guarded. Five soldiers were assigned to make sure she never escaped. One would always be ahead of her, one on each side and two to the rear. She lived every day like this and the guards had strict instructions to shoot her if she showed any sign of trying to escape.

The next morning she awoke as usual and looked around her. Something was different. Her guards were all gone. Only the commander of the guards remained, just standing there a short distance away. As she looked at him, she realised something was wrong with him. He looked distracted, confused, not seeming even to see her. Suddenly she knew the dream was true, this was her day for freedom; the Lord had confused them. After a difficult journey, she eventually was helped to find her way to a transit station for escapees.

Angelina, who had refused to allow the world to forget the Aboke Girls, had a strange phone call in the office of her pressure group. It was from one of the resettlement camps. Someone she didn't know said to her, "Angelina, stand by for some good news. Your daughter Charlotte is here with us."

Angelina was overjoyed and began to sing out her praises to God so loudly that her neighbours wondered what had happened.

A month later, Angelina was able to pass on the same happy news to Phoebe Akelo that her daughter Janet was now free.

She rang Pheobe and said, "Phoebe, do you know God?"

"Yes, I know God."

"Janet is free and on her way home."

Phoebe, with the phone still in her hand cried out at the top of her voice, "God, you are great. Jesus, you are great."

Janet had also sensed that her time had come. She saw the unusual sight of UPDF helicopter gun ships raining down rapid fire from their multi-barrelled machine guns into the LRA camps. She went to her LRA master and asked him to release her. There was the serious possibility that she would also die from the gun-ships firing on the camps where she was staying. At first he shouted at her and said he would not let her go. Undaunted, she continued. She told him that if he allowed her to die in this camp without ever seeing her parents again, his life would never have any peace or success. No matter how evil men become, their God-given conscience still speaks. Fearful that Janet's prediction might become a real curse on his life, and in defiance of strict orders from Kony, he changed his mind and told her to go.

After rest, food and medical checks, the Aboke Girls were flown to Gulu airport for a joyful reunion with their families. The officials had requested the parents to receive their daughters quietly so as not to add to the shock and emotion of their release. But when the girls one by one began to descend the steps from the aircraft, they couldn't help themselves. They began to shout and sing praise to God. They had remained faithful in prayer and trusting that one day God would give them the answer they hoped for. Tears of joy anointed every face. Janet heard a voice shouting praise to God and recognising it as her father, turned and saw him.

Some were just too overcome with emotion, collapsing into the arms of their parents. A local pastor described it as "a resurrection scene." They had been dead and now they were alive. After the great reunion with their parents, the Aboke Girls had one more dramatic and emotional scene to play – their triumphal return to their beloved St Mary's school. As the returnees walked slowly through the gates, some with babies on their hips, the whole school ran to meet them shouting, cheering and singing praise to God who had answered their prayers. Though most of the current students had never met the abductees, they knew each by name and photograph because they had prayed for them individually every day since their abduction.

The sisters of St Mary's knew that release was not enough for their girls. They began to gently speak to them about forgiving their tormentors. This was a hard journey to face, but face it they did. They were taught that they would never be totally free in their hearts until they forgave those who stole their childhood and replaced it with beatings, rape and hunger.

Again Janet has her own testimony. Every memory was like a hard stone in her heart. She asked God, "Please give me your Holy Spirit, but first remove all these stones from my heart."

In response to her deep desire, God came and filled her heart. She began to sing and praise God. Joy filled her for the first time since she had been abducted; she was finally as free in her spirit as she was now, outwardly.

Why did it take so long for the Aboke Girls to be released? With the prayers of so many and the spiritual breakthroughs in their families and churches, surely they could have come home sooner? Theirs was a battle that was part of a war. Outwardly this was a war with guns and oppression, but in reality it was a spiritual war. Such powerful forces of darkness in this world are not easily defeated. Ancient strongholds of powerful witchcraft and tribal hatred had first to be defeated. The slumbering Church had to be awakened to the realities of their own responsibility. It is as if the story of the Aboke Girls was a microcosm of the wider conflict, both physical and, above all, spiritual. It is the one story that has been laid bare for the world to see. The Aboke Girls represent so many others whose story is only fully known by God Himself. Tens of thousands of other children were abducted, and their parents also prayed. For most of them, their story will never be widely known. Their beatings, rape, suffering and in so many cases, death, will not be heard by the outside world or the International Criminal Court. One thing we do know is that the Lord of all the earth and heaven saw it all in its gruesome details and one day judgment will come and it will be an all-knowing and righteous judgement.

Justice Denied

A British Prime Minister, William Gladstone, once famously said, "Justice delayed is justice denied." At the time of writing this book, attempts continue to bring Joseph Kony and his senior commanders to justice. So far he has evaded arrest and trial. Ironically, the man who has given safe refuge to the LRA, Omar Hasan Ahmad al-Bashir, President of the Islamic Republic of Sudan, has himself been named as a perpetrator of "Crimes against humanity" by the International Criminal Court (ICC) for ordering and overseeing the mass murder, rape and displacement of the African population of Darfur.

The ICC indicted Joseph Kony on October 6th 2005, along with a number of his senior commanders. The ICC made a total of thirty three charges. On October 13th, the chief prosecutor, Luis Morano Ocampo, released details of the charges which included twelve crimes against humanity, murder, enslavement, sexual enslavement and rape, and twenty-one counts of war crimes which include murder, cruel treatment of civilians, intentionally directing attacks against the civilian population, pillaging, inducing rape and enforced enlisting of children into the rebel ranks.

Knowing that the indictments were coming, on August 1st Kony met with journalists and said he was not willing to stand trial at the ICC because he claimed, "I have not done anything wrong." He also lied saying, "We don't have any children, we only have combatants."

The Ugandan government had won the military war with the LRA once the spiritual battle had been won. However, the potential for the LRA to continue to cause trouble remains because they have a safe haven in Sudan and currently in the north eastern Congo's lawless Garamba Forest. Kony is still in command of several hundred followers and they retain their arms. They could still mount guerrilla raids, cause death and abduct Ugandan nationals. The Sudan government's fig leaf of a reason for harbouring Kony was that they claimed that he had legitimate political grievances. It had also signed a peace agreement to end their own long running civil war against their own, mostly Christian, people in the south. Southern Sudan is now a semi-autonomous region and the ancient city of Juba is the regional capital. The peace agreement in Southern Sudan is not solid. There are unresolved stresses that could cause the twenty year conflict to flare up again. As always, the real losers will be the ordinary peaceful villagers that inevitably become victims, whatever the political reasons behind them. President Museveni made the wise decision to hold peace talks with the LRA. If Kony signed a peace agreement it would remove any excuse for continuing his guerrilla warfare. In July 2006 peace talks began in Juba with representatives of both sides, under the chairmanship of southern Sudan's Vice-President Riek Machar.

From the outset, the peace process has been dogged by crossed communication lines between Kony and his negotiators. Just as the two negotiating teams thought they were finding a solution, Kony would change his mind or cause confusion. The truth is that he is stalling. He doesn't want to give up his arms or disperse his remaining followers. This would leave him vulnerable to arrest by the ICC and leave him stripped of what small power he has left. He sees his safety in staying hidden in the remote bush area of Eastern Congo.

Eastern Congo is an evil and dangerous place. It is totally lawless and authority only comes from the barrel of an AK47. Three types of people inhabit this area. First, and most powerful are the international opportunists, allied to corrupt politicians, who seek to illegally strip Congo of its mineral wealth. The area is rich in diamonds and cobalt. This wealth is often mined by poor private miners, risking their lives for relatively small reward in getting the wealth out of the ground. Health and safety considerations are a sick joke. Often the labour is slave labour. Countless men and children die in these unsafe and unhealthy mines. The "Mr Big's" and their hired guns are always there to protect their criminal interests. Even President Mugabe of the blighted country of Zimbabwe, which is separated geographically from Congo by four hundred miles of Zambian territory, has mines there under the control of his senior military cohorts. Mr. Mugabe, his family and his cabinet have become extremely rich by stealing hundreds of millions of dollars from their own country's economy over many years. His senior military generals, who are essentially the ones who keep him in power, have obtained their great wealth partly from these diamond mines, granted to them by Mugabe. At one stage, economic journalists estimated that Mugabe was spending millions of dollars a week of his own people's money sending Zimbabwean troops to protect his interests when they were threatened by civil war in that part of the Congo. This is international plundering on a grand scale.

Then there are numerous paramilitary groups of thugs that control various areas of Eastern Congo. These thugs are often tribally or clan based. Their aim is to rob and kill. Most of all they try to rob the poor private miners who risk everything to bring small amounts of wealth out of the ground and sell it on to middlemen for a pittance. The middlemen employ their own protection and through bribing everyone in sight, manage to transport the materials out through Zambia or Tanzania. The wealth is then sold on to apparently "legitimate" multinational companies, usually based in South Africa. These are the "blood diamonds" that have cost a lot more than money to become the fashion accessories for the ladies of the affluent Western world.

Thirdly, there are the remnants of the local population who have not left the area or died from violence or disease. When they can't find miners to rob, the thugs attack villages. When news filters through that a gang is closing in on their village, everyone tries to flee to the bush. Meanwhile the thugs kill anyone they can find, rape any women they catch and torture villagers to tell them where the food is hidden. They often come at harvest time. They strip any valuables from the village and then set it on fire. After they have gone the villagers emerge from hiding to start all over again. A whole generation in Eastern Congo know only fear and periodic flight from rebels – sadly they have not experienced any other way of life than this.

Congo has been classified as a "failed state". This means that the authority of the government does not extend throughout its own territory. There is no effective law and order. The government itself is hopelessly corrupt. Roads, electricity and water supplies are not maintained, there are no public services, hospitals, effective policing or schools. Taxes and border customs are not collected. Almost everything in the country runs on bribes and violence is random and uncontrolled.

It is to the northern part of this vast area that Kony moved to hide, once he felt that his position in Sudan was no longer secure. He and his followers have become just one more vicious group living off and terrorising the remaining villagers in the area.

By 2008 the peace negotiators thought that they had finally arrived at a reasonable agreement that would be acceptable to both sides. Sadly, two years of talks aimed at ending this long-running conflict broke down in April 2008 after Kony failed to appear on the Congolese-Sudanese border to sign a peace deal agreed between his negotiators and those of the Ugandan government. Eight of Kony's own negotiators then gave up in exasperation and left the talks, disillusioned. Caleb Alaka, one of the legal advisors said, "Joseph Kony is the problem. We don't want to be blamed for the failure to bring peace to northern Uganda."

Will Kony and the LRA leadership be brought to account for the unspeakable evil they have perpetrated? The balance of probability is that one day they will. Meanwhile, "Justice delayed is justice denied".

The Widows' Song

Anyone who visits one of Beatrice's widows' conferences in Soroti would first be struck by the numbers – up to five thousand enthusiastic and excited ladies of all ages. At best, their lives are difficult. At worst, they live in abject poverty and face hunger, illness and premature death. Add to this their overwhelming sense of loneliness and abandonment and it is easy to see why they are very excited to be with so many others of similar experience. They have heard about the various projects that can lift them out of destitution and this is their chance to take part in them. Now there is hope, an opportunity for them to regain some of their self respect – a way out of humiliation and discouragement.

Then there is the noise that they can make. It is very loud, but it is also a joyful noise with singing and praising God. When they pray, it is loud and all pray together in that African style which is so unusual in the West. God hears every word from every person, the cacophony of voices does not confuse Him. Once you are accustomed to the wall of sound and the conference moves on to teaching and training, this is where the nuts and bolts of the ministry are revealed. The worship and the prayers are the heart and inspiration that gives faith and hope to destitute women with no future to look forward to. The structure and organisation is what translates the spiritual power into seed, food, milk, cows and goats. Every village has a widows' leader. Every district has a coordinator to supervise these village leaders. Overseeing them is the committee chaired by Beatrice herself. It is the leaders who come for training. As many other widows as can make the journey also turn up. Ladies come who are too sick or too pregnant and certainly too poor to make the journey, which often can be an arduous one. Such is their determination to get there and be part of the most exciting movement they have ever encountered.

Recently the trend has been for multiple conferences in the Teso districts. Just too many want to come. By having regional conferences, more can attend and there is less distance to travel. At the time of writing this, Beatrice had over 30,000 widows on her programme of sustainable self-help. Borrow a cow – return a calf. Borrow a goat – return a kid. It is a simple idea, but it only works through belief and spiritual inspiration. It all came about in answer to Beatrice's prayer and a desperate desire to help her fellow widows. Beatrice had to go through the hardship herself first before her heart was ready to feel the pain of these ladies in such desperate situations. To be able to stand before these women and tell them that she also is a widow, that she too has suffered the loss and experienced the humiliation of being a "mother of problems", is the key to gaining their attention and respect. From them come the knowing nods of understanding. This is no first world charity worker with a university degree and career path, breezing in and out in a Land Cruiser, telling them what they ought to do. This woman is real, her experiences are real and her God is real.

Most importantly, Beatrice brings more than sympathy and understanding. She brings hope. It is the chance of a way out of their depressing existence. That hope is both spiritual and practical. In their culture, which is family, group, village and tribe orientated, they are part of a movement. They have heard that even the President and his wife are praising and promoting their efforts. Humiliation turns to pride and a determination to be one of the success stories of the movement. In a part of the world where countless programmes, initiatives and Western initiated plans have failed to make any real difference, this is something that actually works.

The hospice is also a place of physical and spiritual recovery. It would be a strange hospice in the West that loses half its patients because they recover and go home! Anyone visiting the hospice to talk to the widows will soon discover that they all have a story to tell and it is usually a harrowing one. It would be a hard-hearted person indeed that could listen to them without tears welling up in their eyes and a lump in their throat. They are usually keen to tell their story to anyone who cares to listen. To them it is a matter of both pride and gratitude that they are now well fed, clothed and have a warm bed to sleep in at night.

Now thirty-nine years old, Beatrice has become an important person in Teso and its main town of Soroti. She is no longer one that is shunned as a "mother of problems". Important people listen to and consult her. The President and his wife talk about her and hold her and the widows' ministry up as an example to the rest of the nation. Some would like her to go into politics. She would easily gain a seat in Parliament and eventually become a cabinet member. It is a matter of pride for the Ugandan government that they have modernised out of the traditional male-orientated governance and promoted talented women into government and other places of importance. So far she has rejected this call. She is just too busy following God's leading and fulfilling the call that He made on her life when she was young. She has been faithful to that call because God is faithful. The Bible shows us that God has a special place in His heart for the widow, the orphan and the stranger in our midst.

Beatrice has not become wealthy. She is a person of outstanding integrity. She can be trusted with money, to use it wisely for the purpose for which it was intended. Unfortunately, many people who attain positions of control, with funds passing through their hands, fall to the temptation to siphon some of it off for themselves. Beatrice does not do that. She still lives by faith, trusting God to continue to raise up friends and supporters to meet her considerable expenses. She cannot do a normal salaried job, she is too busy organising her widows. At least she has a rent-free house, but there is still the burden of school fees for her four boys. No doubt later, there will be university fees. From the American NGO she was able to claim some expenses. Serving God by serving her widows is her all consuming passion and her only real interest.

Almost all widows in Africa would like the chance to re-marry. It is natural to want the love, companionship and protection of a husband in their culture. Unfortunately, very few ever have the chance. African men, culturally, only want to marry women who have not yet married and there are too few men in most places so they usually have a choice. Their problem is not finding a wife, it is finding the money for the marriage and the bride price. When asked if she would like to re-marry, she just shyly smiles her magnetic smile and says, "If God wills."

One thing is sure: she is too busy to think about anything other than her present work. She works from morning till night. Her cell phone rings every few minutes. Those who know her well worry that she will burn herself out. But however busy she is, she always takes the time to pray, often through the night with her widows. She knows beyond all doubt that it is God who has done all this. It was God who inspired Paul and Tessa to write and tell her that they would build her a house. They didn't realise that they would also build faith in a young African woman who thought her life had been emptied of all hope. God had spoken to her and even though that word was tested, God came through in the end and honoured His word. Ultimately she believed what God had told her. That faith has borne the amazing fruit that everyone can now observe. God is faithful to all who will listen to Him, believe His word and act upon it. Beatrice is no longer a mother of problems, but now *a mother of hope.*

We hope you enjoyed reading this New Wine book.
For details of other New Wine books
and a wide range of titles from other
Word and Spirit publishers visit our website:
www.newwineministries.co.uk
or e mail us on newwine@xalt.co.uk